New Longman Shakespeare

The Merchant of Venice

William Shakespeare

edited by John O'Connor

Longman

Edinburgh Gate
Harlow, Essex

Introduction

To the student

Shakespeare wrote *The Merchant of Venice* so that it could be performed by actors and enjoyed by audiences. To help you get the most out of the play, this edition includes:
- a complete **script**
- **notes** printed next to the script which explain difficulties and point out important features
- **activities** on the same page which will help you to focus on the scene you are reading
- page-by-page **summaries** of the plot
- **exam questions** after each Act, which will give you practice at the right level
- **background information** about *The Merchant of Venice*, Shakespeare's theatre and the verse he uses
- **advice** on how to set out titles and quotations in your essays.

To the teacher

New Longman Shakespeare has been designed to meet the varied and complex needs of students working throughout the 11–16 age-range.

The textual notes

These have been newly written to provide understandable explanations which are easily located on the page:
- notes are placed next to the text with clear line references
- explanations of more complex words are given in context and help is provided with key imagery and historical reference.

The activities

Activities accompanying the text
These are based on the premise that the text is best enjoyed and understood as a script for performance:

- In addition to a wide variety of reading, writing, listening and speaking activities, students are encouraged to: improvise, learn the script for performance, freeze-frame, rehearse, hot-seat, devise graphs and charts and create various forms of artwork, including storyboards, collages and cartoons.
- To provide a clear structure, activities are placed opposite the section of text to which they refer and come under five headings:
  i **Character reviews** help students to think about the many different aspects of a given character which are presented in the course of the play. There might be as many as twenty of these activities on a single major character.
  ii **Actors' interpretations** draw upon actual performances and ask students to consider comments from actors and directors in film and stage productions.
  iii **Shakespeare's language** activities, focusing on everything from imagery to word-play, enable students to understand how the dramatist's language works to convey the central ideas of the play.
  iv **Plot reviews** help students to keep in mind the essential details of what is happening in the story as well as asking them to consider how the plot is structured.
  v **Themes** are explored according to their predominance in each play.
- 'Serial activities' (Portia 1, ... 2, ... 3, for example) enable students to focus in detail on a single key feature.

In addition, students who find extended tasks on Shakespeare a daunting prospect can combine several of these more focused activities – each in itself free-standing – to form the basis of a fuller piece of work.

2 **Exam-style activities**

At the end of each act – and also at the end of the book – there are activities which require SATs and GCSE style responses and offer opportunities for assessment.

3 **Summative activities**

Thinking about the play as a whole ... is a section which offers a wide range of summative activities suitable for all levels.

Differentiation
Many students using this edition will be approaching Shakespeare for the first time; some might be studying the play for their Key Stage 3 SATs exam; others will be working towards GCSE.

1.1 Venice

Antonio's friends, Salerio and Solanio, ask him why he is sad; they suggest that he might be worried about the safety of his ships and the rich cargoes they carry.

1 **In sooth** in truth

sad *not only unhappy; but also thoughtful and serious*

4 **whereof it is born** what has given rise to it

5 **I am to learn** I am ignorant

6 **want-wit** fool, idiot

7 **I have much ado...myself** I am having trouble knowing who I am

9 **argosies with portly sail** large merchant ships with full, majestic sails

10 **signiors and rich burghers** gentlemen and rich citizens

11 **pageants** *wagons drawn around the streets in pageants, showing spectacular scenes*

12 **overpeer the petty traffickers** look down on the smaller trading ships

13 **curtsy** bow (*as they bob up and down*)

do them reverence show them respect

14 **woven wings** sails

15 **had I...forth** if I were engaged in risky enterprises of that kind

16–17 **The better...abroad** *If Solanio were in Antonio's position, all his thoughts would be about his investments, tied up in ships at sea.*

17 **still** always

18 **where sits the wind** which way the wind is blowing

19 **roads** anchorages

20–22 **And every...sad** Everything that looked like a danger to my enterprises would, without a doubt, cause me unhappiness

23 **ague** fever

26 **flats** sandbanks

27 **Andrew** *the name of a ship*

28–29 **Vailing...burial** bowing down so that the tops of her masts were lower than her hull and kissed the sandbank she was wrecked on

30 **edifice** building

31 **bethink me straight** immediately think about

34 **Enrobe** dress up

Act 1

Scene 1

Venice. A street.

Enter ANTONIO, SALERIO, *and* SOLANIO.

ANTONIO   In sooth, I know not why I am so sad;
It wearies me; you say it wearies you;
But how I caught it, found it, or came by it,
What stuff 't is made of, whereof it is born,
I am to learn;   5
And such a want-wit sadness makes of me
That I have much ado to know myself.

SALERIO   Your mind is tossing on the ocean,
There where your argosies with portly sail,
Like signiors and rich burghers on the flood,   10
Or as it were the pageants of the sea,
Do overpeer the petty traffickers
That curtsy to them, do them reverence,
As they fly by them with their woven wings,

SOLANIO   Believe me, sir, had I such venture forth,   15
The better part of my affections would
Be with my hopes abroad. I should be still
Plucking the grass to know where sits the wind,
Peering in maps for ports, and piers, and roads;
And every object that might make me fear   20
Misfortune to my venture out of doubt
Would make me sad.

SALERIO   My wind cooling my broth
Would blow me to an ague when I thought
What harm a wind too great might do at sea.
I should not see the sandy hour-glass run   25
But I should think of shallows and of flats,
And see my wealthy Andrew docked in sand,
Vailing her high top lower than her ribs
To kiss her burial; should I go to church
And see the holy edifice of stone   30
And not bethink me straight of dangerous rocks,
Which touching but my gentle vessel's side
Would scatter all her spices on the stream,
Enrobe the roaring waters with my silks,

1.1 Venice

Gratiano attempts to cheer Antonio up and advises him not to be one of those people who put on a serious expression and remain silent, merely to look clever and wise.

Activities

Actors' interpretations: 'We leave you now with better company'

When Bassanio, Lorenzo and Gratiano arrive (line 57), Salerio and Solanio take their leave. Why? Act out lines 57–68 in different ways; for example: (a) in a very polite and friendly manner; or (b) as though there were some coldness between Salerio and Solanio on the one hand and Bassanio on the other.

Then discuss the following questions:

- What is the relationship between Antonio and Salerio and Solanio (business associates; close friends; family), and how close are they?
- Why do you think Salerio and Solanio refer to the three arrivals as 'better company' for Antonio and call them his 'worthier friends' (lines 59 and 61)?
- Is Antonio's response (lines 62–64) genuine; or is he pleased to see them go?
- What do you think lies behind Bassanio's comment and Salerio's response (lines 66–68)?

67 **grow exceeding strange** have almost become strangers; *or:* have become distant and unfriendly

68 **We'll make...yours** we'll meet whenever it suits you

74 **You have...world** You take everything much too seriously

75 **They lose...care** People who worry too much lose the enjoyment of life

76 **marvellously** amazingly

81–82 **liver...heart** *In Shakespeare's time people believed that different emotions came from various organs in the body.*

82 **mortifying** (1) causing death; (2) denying someone any pleasure

84 **like his grandsire...alabaster** like a stone statue (*on a tomb*) of one of his ancestors

85 **creep into the jaundice** grow depressed and bitter

86 **peevish** bad-tempered

88 **visages** faces

89 **cream and mantle** turn pale and scummed over like stagnant (**standing**) water

90–92 **And do...conceit** and deliberately go quiet so that people will think they are wise, serious and deeply thoughtful

93 **As who...Oracle** as if they are saying, 'I am The Wise One...'

96 **reputed** said to be

BASSANIO	Good signiors both, when shall we laugh? say, when? You grow exceeding strange; must it be so?
SALERIO	We'll make our leisures to attend on yours.

Exeunt SALERIO *and* SOLANIO.

LORENZO	My Lord Bassanio, since you have found Antonio, We two will leave you, but at dinner-time I pray you have in mind where we must meet.	70
BASSANIO	I will not fail you.	
GRATIANO	You look not well, Signior Antonio. You have too much respect upon the world; They lose it that do buy it with much care. Believe me, you are marvellously changed.	75
ANTONIO	I hold the world but as the world, Gratiano, A stage, where every man must play a part, And mine a sad one.	
GRATIANO	Let me play the fool; With mirth and laughter let old wrinkles come, And let my liver rather heat with wine Than my heart cool with mortifying groans. Why should a man whose blood is warm within Sit like his grandsire, cut in alabaster? Sleep when he wakes? and creep into the jaundice By being peevish? I tell thee what, Antonio, (I love thee, and 't is my love that speaks): There are a sort of men whose visages Do cream and mantle like a standing pond, And do a wilful stillness entertain, With purpose to be dressed in an opinion Of wisdom, gravity, profound conceit, As who should say, "I am Sir Oracle, And when I ope my lips, let no dog bark." O my Antonio, I do know of these That therefore only are reputed wise For saying nothing; when I am very sure, If they should speak, would almost damn those ears	80 85 90 95

1.1 Venice

Bassanio says that he has a plan which will enable him to pay off all his debts; and he begins to tell Antonio about the rich, beautiful and virtuous Portia, who lives in Belmont.

Activities

Shakespeare's language: money, gambling and the law (1)

This play is partly about merchants and money-lenders, who live in a city famous for its trade and for its laws; and partly about a rich young heiress besieged by men who are willing to take a high risk in the hope of gaining her and her wealth. It is not surprising, therefore, that much of the language will be about money, gambling and the law.

Find the following words in Scene 1 and use the notes where you need to check their meanings: venture, merchandise, estate, vendible, means, abridged, rate, debts, gag'd, money, warranty, purse, adventuring, owe, hazard, debtor, richly, undervalued, thrift, fortunes, commodity, sum, credit.

Then draw up a chart with three columns, headed *Money, Gambling* and *The law* and place each word in the appropriate column with the relevant line reference.

Note: (a) some words might go in more than one column; (b) if a word occurs more than once, enter all the line references; (c) save your chart for a later activity.

132 **And from...warranty** and your love gives me the authorisation

133 **unburden** reveal to you

136–137 **And if...honour** if this plan is as honourable as you are

138–139 **My purse...occasions** *Antonio will do anything to help Bassanio.*

138 **my extremist means** anything I have or can do

140 **shaft** arrow

141 **his fellow...flight** an arrow of the same size and weight

142 **advisèd** deliberate, careful

144 **I urge...proof** I am offering this truth, based on childhood experience

150–151 **or...or** either...or...

151 **latter hazard** second 'stake'

152 **And thankfully...first** and gratefully remain in your debt for the first one

153–154 **and herein...circumstance** and you are wasting time, beating about the bush like this

156 **making question...uttermost** doubting I'll give you all I have

160 **prest unto it** willing to do it

165–166 **nothing undervalued...Portia** *Bassanio compares her with another Portia, wife of Brutus, (see Shakespeare's* Julius Cæsar, *2.1.294–296).*

169 **Renownèd suitors** *famous men who want to marry Portia*

sunny locks blonde hair

And from your love I have a warranty
To unburden all my plots and purposes
How to get clear of all the debts I owe.

ANTONIO   I pray you, good Bassanio, let me know it,   135
And if it stand, as you yourself still do,
Within the eye of honour, be assured
My purse, my person, my extremest means
Lie all unlocked to your occasions.

BASSANIO   In my school-days, when I had lost one shaft,   140
I shot his fellow of the self-same flight
The self-same way, with more advisèd watch,
To find the other forth, and by adventuring both,
I oft found both; I urge this childhood proof
Because what follows is pure innocence.   145
I owe you much, and, like a wilful youth,
That which I owe is lost, but if you please
To shoot another arrow that self way
Which you did shoot the first, I do not doubt,
As I will watch the aim, or to find both,   150
Or bring your latter hazard back again,
And thankfully rest debtor for the first.

ANTONIO   You know me well, and herein spend but time
To wind about my love with circumstance,
And out of doubt you do me now more wrong   155
In making question of my uttermost
Than if you had made waste of all I have.
Then do but say to me what I should do
That in your knowledge may by me be done,
And I am prest unto it: therefore speak.   160

BASSANIO   In Belmont is a lady richly left,
And she is fair, and, fairer than that word,
Of wondrous virtues. Sometimes from her eyes
I did receive fair speechless messages.
Her name is Portia, nothing undervalued   165
To Cato's daughter, Brutus' Portia,
Nor is the wide world ignorant of her worth,
For the four winds blow in from every coast
Renownèd suitors, and her sunny locks
Hang on her temples like a golden fleece,   170

1.2 Belmont: Portia's house

Portia is depressed because her dead father's will prevents her from choosing a husband; instead, any man who wants to marry her has to pick one of three caskets – gold, silver or lead: whoever chooses the right one will become her husband. Nerissa begins to describe the current suitors.

Activities

Shakespeare's language: money, gambling and the law (2)

Look back at the activity on page 10 and the chart you drew up. Add the examples of legal language found here in Portia's comment about the Englishman and the Scotsman (lines 68–82).

The following example of legal language comes from Shakespeare's own will. It begins:

> *In the name of God Amen. I William Shackspeare of Stratford upon Avon in the county of Warwickshire gent., in perfect health & memory God be praised, do make & ordain this my last will & testament in manner & form following. That is to say first...*

Later he writes:

> *Item. I give unto my wife my second best bed with the furniture.*

Notes: (a) he did spell his name like that in his will; (b) *gent* means that he was a gentleman by rank; (c) the word *Item* used to be placed in front of points on a list.)

Use this example to draw up the will written by Portia's father, which includes the crucial clause about the caskets (lines 28–36).

17–21 **the brain...cripple** although we create commonsense rules to control our emotions (**blood**), we break them in moments of passion: young people are impetuous and ignore restraining wise advice

22 **in the fashion** the kind of thing

24–25 **the will...curbed** the wishes...thwarted (**will** = [1] wishes; [2] the legal document)

31–32 **whereof who...meaning** in which the man who understands the meaning correctly

37 **over-name them** read out their names

39 **level at** guess at; work out

40 **Neapolitan** from Naples

41 **colt** (1) young male horse; (2) immature boy

42–43 **he makes it...parts** he is really proud that one of his talents is

45 **played false** had an affair

46 **County Palatine** the Count of the Palatine

47 **as who should say** as if to say

50 **weeping philosopher** *the Greek Heraclitus, who wept at men's foolishness*

51 **unmannerly** inappropriate

52 **death's-head** *the skull and crossed bones frequently carved on tomb-stones*

twenty what were good to be done than be one of
the twenty to follow mine own teaching; the
brain may devise laws for the blood, but a hot
temper leaps o'er a cold decree – such a hare is
madness the youth, to skip o'er the meshes of   20
good counsel the cripple. But this reasoning is
not in the fashion to choose me a husband. O
me, the word "choose"! I may neither choose who
I would, nor refuse who I dislike, so is the will of a
living daughter curbed by the will of a dead   25
father. Is it not hard, Nerissa, that I cannot choose
one, nor refuse none?

NERISSA   Your father was ever virtuous, and holy men at
their death have good inspirations; therefore the
lottery that he hath devised in these three chests,   30
of gold, silver, and lead, whereof who chooses his
meaning chooses you, will no doubt never be
chosen by any rightly, but one who you shall
rightly love. But what warmth is there in your
affection towards any of these princely suitors that 35
are already come?

PORTIA   I pray thee over-name them, and as thou namest
them, I will describe them. And according to my
description level at my affection.

NERISSA   First there is the Neapolitan prince.   40

PORTIA   Ay, that's a colt indeed, for he doth nothing but
talk of his horse, and he makes it a great
appropriation to his own good parts that he can
shoe him himself. I am much afeared my lady his
mother played false with a smith.   45

NERISSA   Then is there the County Palatine.

PORTIA   He doth nothing but frown, as who should say,
"an you will not have me, choose". He hears merry
tales and smiles not; I fear he will prove the
weeping philosopher when he grows old, being   50
so full of unmannerly sadness in his youth. I had
rather be married to a death's-head with a bone in

1.2 Belmont: Portia's house

Much to Portia's relief, Nerissa finally reveals that all the suitors they have been discussing have decided to pull out of the contest and return home. Portia has fond memories of a young Venetian who once visited the house, called Bassanio.

Activities

Actors' interpretations: 'Yes, yes, it was Bassanio'

A Can you tell what Portia really feels about Bassanio from lines 116–121? In pairs, decide whether she can hardly recall his name or remembers him very well.

B Some actresses say 'Yes, yes, it was Bassanio' very excitedly; then, realising that they have revealed their feelings, they stop and add 'as I think so was he called' pretending that they can barely remember the man!

In pairs, try performing the lines in that way. Then act out the dialogue quite differently – as though Portia genuinely has only a slight recollection of Bassanio.

Which interpretation works best, in your opinion, bearing in mind what you have learned about Portia?

C Write Portia's diary entry, in which she records her conversation with Nerissa and her mention of Bassanio.

89–90 **An the worst...fell** If the worst thing that could ever happen does happen...

90 **make shift** manage

95 **Rhenish** *from the Rhineland in Germany*

contrary wrong

98 **ere** before

99 **sponge** *someone who drinks too much*

101 **acquainted me...determinations** informed me of their decisions

103 **suit** wooing

104–105 **by some other sort...imposition** by some other method than your father's command (*in his will*)

107 **Sibylla** *a Greek prophetess, granted long life by Apollo*

chaste as Diana *Diana was the Roman goddess of virginity.*

109 **parcel** bunch

111 **dote on** love excessively

115 **hither** here

Montferrat *a famous Italian family*

| | beast. An the worst fall that ever fell, I hope I shall make shift to go without him. | 90 |

NERISSA　If he should offer to choose, and choose the right casket, you should refuse to perform your father's will, if you should refuse to accept him.

PORTIA　Therefore, for fear of the worst, I pray thee set a deep glass of Rhenish wine on the contrary 95 casket, for if the devil be within, and that temptation without, I know he will choose it. I will do anything, Nerissa, ere I will be married to a sponge.

NERISSA　You need not fear, lady, the having any of these 100 lords; they have acquainted me with their determinations, which is, indeed, to return to their home, and to trouble you with no more suit, unless you may be won by some other sort than your father's imposition, depending on the 105 caskets.

PORTIA　If I live to be as old as Sibylla, I will die as chaste as Diana, unless I be obtained by the manner of my father's will. I am glad this parcel of wooers are so reasonable, for there is not one among 110 them but I dote on his very absence; and I pray God grant them a fair departure.

NERISSA　Do you not remember, lady, in your father's time, a Venetian, a scholar and a soldier, that came hither in company of the Marquis of Montferrat? 115

PORTIA　Yes, yes, it was Bassanio, as I think so was he called.

NERISSA　True, madam, he of all the men that ever my foolish eyes looked upon was the best deserving a fair lady.

PORTIA　I remember him well, and I remember him worthy 120 of thy praise.

Enter a SERVING-MAN.

How now, what news?

1.3 Venice

Shylock expresses some concerns about the safety of Antonio's investments, but agrees to think seriously about entering into a contract to lend him the money. When Antonio arrives, Shylock tells the audience how much he hates him and why, vowing that he will get his revenge if he can.

15–16 he is sufficient he has enough money to repay the loan

16 his means are in supposition there are some doubts about his finances

17–18 Tripolis…Indies Tripoli (*in present-day Lebanon*) and the East Indies

18 the Rialto *the exchange where Venetian merchants met to discuss business*

20 squandered scattered

25 notwithstanding despite all that

26 take his bond accept the legal contract he is offering

27 assured *Bassanio means 'you can feel reassured that the contract is a sound one'; Shylock replies that he will certainly obtain financial 'assurance' (guarantees).*

29 bethink me think about it carefully

31 pork *a meat which Jews are forbidden to eat for religious reasons*

habitation dwelling-place

32 your prophet…into *Jews revered Jesus of Nazareth as a prophet, but not the son of God; Shylock refers to the story in the Bible in which devils driven out of two madmen by Jesus entered pigs.*

38 fawning flattering ('a creep')

publican (1) tax-collector (*Roman tax-gatherers had oppressed Jews in Biblical times*); (2) inn-keeper

39 for because

40 in low simplicity naively

41 gratis free (*i.e. without charging interest*)

42 usance interest (*connected with 'usury' – money-lending – see page 202*)

43 catch him…hip get him at a disadvantage (*a wrestling term*)

44 feed fat satisfy to the full

45 sacred nation the Jewish people (*also my tribe – lines 48 and 54*)

rails insults me with abusive language

47 thrift money acquired by careful management (*see line 86*)

SHYLOCK	Ho no, no, no, no; my meaning in saying he is a good man is to have you understand me that he is sufficient. Yet his means are in supposition; he hath an argosy bound to Tripolis, another to the Indies. I understand, moreover, upon the Rialto, he hath a third at Mexico, a fourth for England, and other ventures he hath squandered abroad. But ships are but boards, sailors but men; there be land-rats and water-rats, water-thieves, and land-thieves, (I mean pirates), and then there is the peril of waters, winds, and rocks; the man is, notwithstanding, sufficient. Three thousand ducats – I think I may take his bond.

15

20

25

BASSANIO   Be assured you may.

SHYLOCK   I *will* be assured I may; and, that I may be assured,
            I will bethink me. May I speak with Antonio?

BASSANIO   If it please you to dine with us.   30

SHYLOCK   Yes, to smell pork, to eat of the habitation which
            your prophet the Nazarite conjured the devil into.
            I will buy with you, sell with you, talk with you,
            walk with you, and so following, but I will not eat
            with you, drink with you, nor pray with you. What   35
            news on the Rialto? Who is he comes here?

            Enter ANTONIO.

BASSANIO   This is Signior Antonio.

SHYLOCK   (*Aside*)
            How like a fawning publican he looks!
            I hate him for he is a Christian:
            But more, for that in low simplicity   40
            He lends out money gratis, and brings down
            The rate of usance here with us in Venice.
            If I can catch him once upon the hip,
            I will feed fat the ancient grudge I bear him.
            He hates our sacred nation, and he rails,   45
            Even there where merchants most do congregate,
            On me, my bargains, and my well-won thrift,
            Which he calls interest; cursed be my tribe

1.3 Venice

Antonio cannot see why the Jacob story supports the idea that taking interest is acceptable, and he insults Shylock. In response to Antonio's harsh words, Shylock reminds the merchant how badly he has treated him in the past.

Activities

Character review: Shylock (2)

His humour and wit
When David Suchet played Shylock in 1981, he said, 'Antonio's visit is a situation with a good deal of humour for Shylock, and I wanted, when I played the part, to bring it out as effectively as possible.' Philip Voss (1997) and Henry Goodman (1999) also brought out Shylock's humour.

In pairs, act out the following exchanges to try to bring out Shylock's humour or his quick-wittedness and ability to find a sharp reply:
- lines 21–23: 'But ships...pirates' (pirats!)
- lines 30–32: 'If it...into.'
- lines 49–53: 'Shylock, do...ducats;'
- lines 91–93: 'Was this...fast –'

Draw a series of cartoon frames to illustrate the story Shylock tells about Jacob and Laban (lines 68–85). At the end, explain the 'message' of the story in your own words.

78 **turnèd to** went to mate with
79 **work of generation** the act of mating
81 **pilled me...wands** cut some sticks and peeled off the bark
82 **in the doing...kind** during the act of mating
83 **fulsome** *perhaps* lustful, fertile *or* pregnant
84 **eaning** lambing
85 **Fall** give birth to
   parti-coloured black and white
86 **thrive** succeed financially
88 **served** worked
90 **swayed and fashioned** influenced and brought about
91 **inserted** introduced
   good acceptable
95–96 **cite Scripture** quote examples from the Bible (*compare* **producing holy witness**)
101 **rate** rate of interest
102 **beholding** in debt
104 **rated** berated; criticised (*with a possible pun on* **rate**, *line 101*)
   usances money-lending
106 **Still** always
107 **sufferance** putting up with things (*'suffering'*)
   badge distinguishing mark
108 **misbeliever** *someone who believes in a false religion*
109 **gaberdine** *loose cloak*

In end of autumn turnèd to the rams,
And when the work of generation was
Between these woolly breeders in the act,   80
The skilful shepherd pilled me certain wands,
And in the doing of the deed of kind
He stuck them up before the fulsome ewes,
Who, then conceiving, did in eaning time
Fall parti-coloured lambs, and those were Jacob's   85
This was a way to thrive, and he was blest;
And thrift is blessing if men steal it not.

ANTONIO   This was a venture, sir, that Jacob served for,
A thing not in his power to bring to pass,
But swayed and fashioned by the hand of heaven.   90
Was this inserted to make interest good?
Or is your gold and silver ewes and rams?

SHYLOCK   I cannot tell, I make it breed as fast –
But note me, signior …

ANTONIO   Mark you this, Bassanio,
The devil can cite Scripture for his purpose;   95
An evil soul producing holy witness
Is like a villain with a smiling cheek,
A goodly apple rotten at the heart.
O what a goodly outside falsehood hath!

SHYLOCK   Three thousand ducats, 't is a good round sum.   100
Three months from twelve – then let me see the
            rate.

ANTONIO   Well, Shylock, shall we be beholding to you?

SHYLOCK   Signior Antonio, many a time and oft
In the Rialto you have rated me
About my moneys and my usances.   105
Still have I borne it with a patient shrug,
For sufferance is the badge of all our tribe.
You call me misbeliever, cut-throat dog,
And spit upon my Jewish gaberdine,
And all for use of that which is mine own.   110
Well then, it now appears you need my help.
Go to, then, you come to me, and you say,
"Shylock, we would have moneys"; you say so;

1.3 Venice

Antonio angrily replies to Shylock's accusation, but seems happy to accept a proposal. Shylock is willing to lend the money and take no interest; but, if Antonio does not repay the loan on time, Shylock can cut off a pound of the merchant's flesh!

Activities

Character review: Shylock (3)

'Signior Antonio…'
Re-read Shylock's reply to Antonio (lines 103–126).

A List the things that Antonio has done to Shylock in public and describe how Shylock has reacted (lines 103–110). How does Shylock feel now that Antonio comes to him to borrow money (lines 111–126)?

B In small groups, freeze-frame some of the examples of Antonio's behaviour that Shylock describes (lines 103–110). Compare your freeze-frames with other groups' and talk about the kinds of emotions which can be seen in the characters' faces. Then create a single freeze-frame to represent Shylock's response (lines 111–126).

C Act out Shylock's reply in as many different ways as you can: with humour, anger, sarcasm, bitterness… First pick out the key words (rated, usances, sufferance…). You might then decide that Shylock's tone changes several times in the course of the speech. How does it end, for example? Are the final four lines bitter or good-humoured?

114 **void your rheum** spit out phlegm

115–116 **foot me…threshold** kick me, as though throwing a stray dog off your property

116 **moneys is your suit** you are asking for money

120 **bondman's key** slave's tone of voice

121 **bated breath** soft, respectful voice

130–131 **when did…friend?** when did friends ever take interest off each other?

133 **if he break** if he breaks the contract (*by failing to pay the money back on time*); *or:* if he becomes bankrupt

133–134 **thou may'st…penalty** it will look better when you make him pay the penalty

135 **would be** would like to be

137–138 **no doit Of usance** not a penny in interest

139 **kind** (1) kindness; (2) a natural offer that anyone might make

141 **notary** lawyer

141–142 **seal me…bond** sign and seal this simple contract, without conditions (**single bond**)

142 **merry sport** joke

145 **forfeit** penalty

146 **nominated for** named as

equal exact

149 **Content, in faith** I'm certainly happy with that

1.3

You that did void your rheum upon my beard,
And foot me as you spurn a stranger cur   115
Over your threshold; moneys is your suit.
What should I say to you? Should I not say:
"Hath a dog money? Is it possible
A cur can lend three thousand ducats?"; or
Shall I bend low, and in a bondman's key,   120
With bated breath and whispering humbleness
Say this:
"Fair sir, you spat on me on Wednesday last;
You spurned me such a day; another time
You called me dog; and for these courtesies   125
I'll lend you thus much moneys"?

ANTONIO   I am as like to call thee so again,
To spit on thee again, to spurn thee too.
If thou wilt lend this money, lend it not
As to thy friends, for when did friendship take   130
A breed for barren metal of his friend?
But lend it rather to thine enemy,
Who if he break, thou may'st with better face
Exact the penalty.

SHYLOCK   Why, look you, how you storm!
I would be friends with you, and have your love,   135
Forget the shames that you have stained me with,
Supply your present wants, and take no doit
Of usance for my moneys, and you'll not hear me –
This is kind I offer.

BASSANIO   This were kindness.

SHYLOCK   This kindness will I show.   140
Go with me to a notary; seal me there
Your single bond, and, in a merry sport,
If you repay me not on such a day,
In such a place, such sum or sums as are
Expressed in the condition, let the forfeit   145
Be nominated for an equal pound
Of your fair flesh, to be cut off and taken
In what part of your body pleaseth me.

ANTONIO   Content, in faith; I'll seal to such a bond,
And say there is much kindness in the Jew.   150

Bassanio is uneasy about the terms of the agreement, but Antonio accepts it and reassures Bassanio: his ships are expected back a month before the repayment date.

Activities

Character review: Shylock (4)

The bond
Does Shylock offer the bond in a genuine attempt to gain Antonio's friendship; or is it part of a deliberate plot to bring about the merchant's downfall? Look back through the scene and grade each of the following interpretations from 1 (I strongly disagree) to 5 (I strongly agree). Then argue for your preferred interpretations in a class discussion:

- Shylock sees the bond as his chance to trap Antonio and get even with him (Bob Peck, 1996).
- He treats the bond as another joke (Philip Voss, 1997).
- He is simply mocking Antonio and humiliating him when he adds the flesh clause (Patrick Stewart, 1978).
- He offers the bond genuinely in the hope of gaining the Christians' friendship and joining their circle (Laurence Olivier, 1973).
- He is fed up with all the past hatred and offers the bond as a sincere way of starting afresh (Henry Goodman, 1999).

152 **dwell in my necessity** remain in need of the money

153 **forfeit it** break the contract by failing to repay the money

160 **break his day** miss the deadline for repaying the loan

161 **exaction of the forfeiture** carrying out the penalty

163 **estimable** valuable

166 **If he...adieu** if he will accept this offer – fine; if not, goodbye

170 **direction** instructions

171 **purse the ducats straight** collect the money straightaway (*but compare lines 50–55*)

172 **fearful** causing anxiety (*because the servant is careless:* **unthrifty**, *line 173*)

173 **presently** straightaway

174 **Hie thee** make haste; hurry

gentle (1) kind and 'gentlemanly'; (2) *a pun on* 'gentile' *(non-Jewish)*

176 **fair terms** a fair deal

177 **dismay** danger

1.3

BASSANIO	You shall not seal to such a bond for me;
	I'll rather dwell in my necessity.
ANTONIO	Why, fear not, man, I will not forfeit it
	Within these two months, that's a month before
	This bond expires, I do expect return 155
	Of thrice three times the value of this bond.
SHYLOCK	O father Abram, what these Christians are,
	Whose own hard dealings teaches them suspect
	The thoughts of others! Pray you, tell me this:
	If he should break his day, what should I gain 160
	By the exaction of the forfeiture?
	A pound of man's flesh taken from a man
	Is not so estimable, profitable neither.
	As flesh of muttons, beefs, or goats. I say,
	To buy his favour I extend this friendship; 165
	If he will take it, so; if not, adieu,
	And for my love I pray you wrong me not.
ANTONIO	Yes, Shylock, I will seal unto this bond.
SHYLOCK	Then meet me forthwith at the notary's.
	Give him direction for this merry bond, 170
	And I will go and purse the ducats straight,
	See to my house, left in the fearful guard
	Of an unthrifty knave; and presently
	I'll be with you.

Exit.

ANTONIO	Hie thee, gentle Jew.
	(*To* BASSANIO) The Hebrew will turn Christian, he
	grows kind. 175
BASSANIO	I like not fair terms and a villain's mind.
ANTONIO	Come on, in this there can be no dismay;
	My ships come home a month before the day.

Exeunt.

Exam practice

Character review: the end of the Act

Look again at 1.3.169–178. Read what is said by each character and think carefully about what they are really thinking or feeling.

Your task is to produce the sub-text of this scene. Copy out Shakespeare's lines and then write down what each character is really thinking or feeling beside the actual text.

Themes: anti-Semitism (1)

Shylock is Jew; and, before looking further at the way he is treated by the Christians in the play, it is important to understand something about the history of anti-Semitism – the irrational hatred and persecution of Jews. Read the section on pages 200–202 and then, as a class, brainstorm your knowledge about anti-Semitism. What do you know about the Holocaust, for example? Have you seen *Schindler's List*? Why were Jews persecuted in the Middle Ages and unjustly viewed with suspicion in Shakespeare's lifetime?

To check that you understand their feelings for one another, write lists of all the reasons why (a) Antonio hates Shylock; and (b) Shylock hates Antonio. Look at what they say to each other and think about the things that have happened between them before their meeting in 1.3.

Shakespeare's language: word-play (1)

Shakespeare loved word-play, especially punning on the word 'will'.
1. How many meanings of 'will' can you think of in modern English (with and without a capital W)? Use a dictionary to check your list.
2. Why do you think Shakespeare might have been so fond of this particular pun? (Have a look at his Sonnet 135; you can find it in a 'Complete Works' of Shakespeare.)
3. What might Portia mean by 'so is the will of a living daughter curbed by the will of a dead father' 1.2.24–25? How many meanings of 'will' can you find in that sentence? What effect do these 'wills' have on Portia's life?

Character review: Antonio (2)

'A stage, where every man must play a part...'
1. Shakespeare often compares people to actors, as in *As You Like It* (2.7):
      All the world's a stage,
      And all the men and women merely players...
   What is Antonio's version of this idea? (1.1.77–79) How would you put it in your own words? What does it tell you about his personality and his attitude to life?
2. What is your impression of Antonio after seeing him with Shylock? Make two lists: one of all the things you like or admire in Antonio and another of all the things you dislike or disapprove of. Find a quotation to back up each point. Then write two paragraphs: one 'for' and one 'against' Antonio.

Character review: Bassanio (2)

What do you think of him?
Write a further page of Salerio's letter to Solanio (see page 12) in which you add your opinions of Bassanio.
1. First comment on his actions:
   (a) Do you think Bassanio's plan to marry Portia is a good one?
   (b) Is it fair of him to ask Antonio for another loan when he already owes him a great deal?
2. Then give your views on Bassanio's character:
   (a) Is Bassanio simply careless with money, or a spoilt rich boy?
   (b) Is he a genuine friend to Antonio, or a scrounger?
   (c) When he starts to describe Portia, the first phrase he uses is 'richly left'; then he adds that she is 'fair' and 'of wondrous virtues'. Do you think that he is only after her money?
   Make sure that you find points in the play to support your opinions.

Actors' interpretations: reactions

Actors have to think carefully about what they do while other characters are speaking.
1. What do Bassanio and Antonio do during Shylock's aside (1.3.38–49)?
2. How do they react during his story about Jacob and Laban (1.3.73–87)?
3. How does Bassanio react while Antonio is accepting Shylock's offer of the bond (1.3.140–150)?

Actors' interpretations: Shylock's accent

Do you think Shylock should be played with a noticeable accent? Antony Sher (1987) had a Turkish accent; Ian McDiarmid (1984) sounded German; Patrick Stewart (1978) was very 'refined'; David Calder (1993) used his own Received Pronunciation; Laurence Olivier's Shylock (1973) tried to sound like the Christians, but did not quite make it; Warren Mitchell (BBC, 1980) was accused of sounding like a stereotype of a comic stage Jew.

In each case, the actor chose an accent to fit the character he had created and the place and period in which his interpretation was set. Try speaking some of Shylock's speeches in different accents and types of voice, and decide which sounds right. But, whatever you do, make sure you do not simply mock the way he speaks.

Themes: appearance and reality (1)

A theme is an important subject which seems to be treated in various ways throughout the play. Themes in *The Merchant of Venice* include: anti-Semitism; justice and mercy; Venice and Belmont; true and false values; Jews and Christians; love and hate; appearance and reality.

Shakespeare's plays often ask us to think about the idea that appearances can be deceptive: things are not always what they seem. Re-read Antonio's speech (1.3.94–99).
1. How many other 'smiling villains' can you think of – people whose friendly looks disguise their evil – in drama, fiction, television, film or real life?
2. Do you think Shylock deserves these harsh words?
3. Which other moments in Act 1 seem to be connected to the theme of appearance and reality?

2.1 Belmont: Portia's house

In Belmont, Portia meets her next suitor, the Prince of Morocco.

s.d. **a tawny Moor** *Black people in Shakespeare's time were usually called 'moors' (whether they came from Morocco itself or other parts of Africa); tawny suggests a lighter skin colouring than deep black.*

accordingly looking the same

1 **Mislike me not** do not dislike me

complexion (1) the mixture of 'humours' which make up somebody's personality; (2) skin colour

2 **shadowed livery** dark-coloured uniform (*his black skin*)

burnished polished up and shiny

3 **near bred** close relative (*they are both great and powerful*)

5 **Phoebus' fire** the sun's heat (*Phoebus was the classical sun-god*)

6 **make incision** cut ourselves to draw blood

7 **reddest** redness was a sign of courage and nobility

8 **aspect** appearance

9 **feared the valiant** frightened brave men

10 **best-regarded** most admired

clime climate; country

11 **hue** colour

13 **In terms of choice** as far as choice goes

14 **by nice...eyes** by the over-fussy way in which young women judge by appearances

15–16 **the lottery...choosing** the game of chance on which my fate depends does not permit me to choose for myself

17 **scanted** restricted

18–19 **hedged me...His wife...** confined me in his wisdom to give myself as a wife to whoever...

20 **renownèd** famous

as fair (1) with as fair a chance; (2) with as fair a skin

24 **scimitar** kind of curved sword

25 **Sophy** Emperor of Persia

26 **three fields of** three battles against

27 **o'erstare** outstare

31 **alas the while!** a common expression of regret

32 **Hercules and Lichas** a Greek hero, famous for his strength (also called **Alcides**, line 35), and his servant

Act 2

Scene 1

Belmont. A room in Portia's house.

A florish of cornets. Enter the Prince of MOROCCO, *a tawny Moor, all
in white, and three or four followers accordingly, with* PORTIA,
NERISSA, *and their train.*

MOROCCO   Mislike me not for my complexion,
The shadowed livery of the burnished sun,
To whom I am a neighbour, and near bred.
Bring me the fairest creature northward born,
Where Phœbus' fire scarce thaws the icicles,   5
And let us make incision for your love,
To prove whose blood is reddest, his or mine.
I tell thee, lady, this aspect of mine
Hath feared the valiant; by my love I swear,
The best-regarded virgins of our clime   10
Have loved it too. I would not change this hue,
Except to steal your thoughts, my gentle queen.

PORTIA   In terms of choice I am not solely led
By nice direction of a maiden's eyes;
Besides, the lottery of my destiny   15
Bars me the right of voluntary choosing;
But if my father had not scanted me,
And hedged me by his wit to yield myself
His wife, who wins me by that means I told you,
Your self, renownèd prince, then stood as fair   20
As any comer I have looked on yet
For my affection.

MOROCCO   Even for that I thank you;
Therefore I pray you lead me to the caskets
To try my fortune. By this scimitar
That slew the Sophy, and a Persian prince   25
That won three fields of Sultan Solyman,
I would o'erstare the sternest eyes that look,
Outbrave the heart most daring on the earth,
Pluck the young sucking cubs from the she-bear,
Yea, mock the lion when he roars for prey,   30
To win thee, lady. But alas the while!
If Hercules and Lichas play at dice,
Which is the better man, the greater throw

2.2 Near Shylock's house

Portia reminds Morocco that, if he chooses the wrong casket, he must never propose marriage to any other woman; he agrees and they depart for the temple. Back in Venice, Shylock's servant, Launcelot Gobbo, is torn between staying with his master or running away.

Activities

Character review: Morocco (1)

Comic or serious?

A What kind of person do you think Morocco is? Try to find examples from what he says and does which suggest that he might be: boastful; a show-off; macho; conceited; good-looking; rich; powerful.

B Morocco is often played as a comic character – very overdone and boastful. But in the 1999 Royal National Theatre production, Morocco (as played by Chu Omambala) was a very dignified young man, to whom Portia became attracted.
1. Read the scene in pairs, picking out evidence in the script which suggests (a) a comic interpretation, and (b) a more serious approach.
2. Then act the scene, first making Morocco comically melodramatic and conceited, then playing him seriously so that Portia becomes genuinely attracted to him.
   Which of the two approaches seems to work best, in your opinion?

C Improvise a discussion between a director, who feels that Morocco has to be played comically, and an actor who believes that to do so would result in a racist interpretation.

42 **be advised** think about this carefully

44 **temple** *the chapel where each suitor must swear to abide by the rules*

45 **hazard** *decision involving chance*

46 **cursed'st** most cursed

s.d. **clown** *The main comic character in Shakespeare's plays was often listed as 'clown'.*

1 **serve** allow

2 **the fiend** the devil

6 **take heed** be careful

9 **scorn** reject

10 **pack** run away
   "Fia!" 'Go on!'

13–14 **hanging about...heart** clinging to my heart for comfort

> May turn by fortune from the weaker hand;
> So is Alcides beaten by his page,   35
> And so may I, blind Fortune leading me,
> Miss that which one unworthier may attain,
> And die with grieving.

PORTIA   You must take your chance,
And either not attempt to choose at all,
Or swear before you choose, if you choose
    wrong,   40
Never to speak to lady afterward
In way of marriage; therefore be advised.

MOROCCO   Nor will not. Come, bring me unto my chance.

PORTIA   First, forward to the temple; after dinner
Your hazard shall be made.

MOROCCO   Good fortune then,   45
To make me blest or cursed'st among men!

Sound of cornets. Exeunt.

Scene 2

Venice. A street.

Enter LAUNCELOT GOBBO, *the clown, alone.*

LAUNCELOT   Certainly, my conscience will serve me to run from
this Jew my master; the fiend is at mine elbow, and
tempts me, saying to me. "Gobbo, Launcelot
Gobbo, good Launcelot," or "good Gobbo", or
"good Launcelot Gobbo, use your legs, take the   5
start, run away." My conscience says, "No; take
heed, honest Launcelot, take heed, honest Gobbo,"
or, as aforesaid, "honest Launcelot Gobbo; do not
run, scorn running with thy heels." Well, the most
courageous fiend bids me pack, "Fia!" says the   10
fiend, "away!" says the fiend, "for the heavens,
rouse up a brave mind," says the fiend, "and run."
Well, my conscience, hanging about the neck of my
heart, says very wisely to me: "My honest friend
Launcelot" – being an honest man's son, or rather   15

2.2 Near Shylock's house

Just as he decides to leave Shylock's service, Launcelot's old father approaches. He is almost blind and Launcelot decides to play a trick on him.

Activities

Character review: Launcelot Gobbo (1)

Talking to the audience
Re-read Launcelot Gobbo's speech (lines 1–31).

A What exactly is the problem that he is trying to sort out? Why is he so torn? Do you think he ends up making the right choice?

B Redraft Launcelot's speech as a playscript with three characters: Launcelot, his conscience and 'the fiend'. Include stage directions (such as *tugging at his elbow*, line 3) and advice on how lines are spoken. Then perform the dialogue in groups of three, choosing contrasting voices and appropriate movements for the three characters.

C Decide how Launcelot's speech ought to be acted in a performance of the play and annotate the script accordingly. (Perhaps it ought to be kept simple; Christopher Luscombe, who played the part in 1993, offered the advice: 'DON'T work out a gag for every single line!')

17–18 **something smack...grow to...taste** *All these expressions mean 'he was inclined to...he had a touch of...' and imply that he was sexually promiscuous.*

21 **counsel well** give good advice

23 **God bless the mark** may God forgive me (*an apologetic oath, like* **saving your reverence**, *line 25*)

27 **incarnation** *a malapropism; he means 'incarnate' (= in the flesh; in human form)*

34 **true-begotten** true-born (*another mistake: people usually talk about a true-begotten child*)

35 **sand-blind** *This is from an old expression 'sam-blind' ('sam' = 'semi', i.e. half blind); Launcelot invents gravel-blind as an even worse state.*

36 **confusions** *another malapropism: he means 'conclusions' (riddles)*

43 **sonties** saints

hit find

47 **raise the waters** make him cry

an honest woman's son, for indeed my father did
something smack, something grow to; he had a
kind of taste – well, my conscience says "Launcelot,
budge not!" "Budge!" says the fiend. "Budge not!"
says my conscience. "Conscience," say I, "you   20
counsel well; fiend," say I, "you counsel well"; to
be ruled by my conscience, I should stay with the
Jew my master, who (God bless the mark) is a kind
of devil; and to run away from the Jew I should be
ruled by the fiend, who (saving your reverence) is   25
the devil himself; certainly the Jew is the very devil
incarnation, and in my conscience, my conscience
is but a kind of hard conscience, to offer to counsel
me to stay with the Jew; the fiend gives the more
friendly counsel: I will run, fiend; my heels are at   30
your commandment; I will run.

Enter old GOBBO *with a basket.*

GOBBO   Master young man, you I pray you, which is the
             way to Master Jew's?

LAUNCELOT   (*Aside*)
             O heavens! this is my true-begotten father, who,
             being more than sand-blind, high gravel-blind,   35
             knows me not. I will try confusions with him.

GOBBO   Master young gentleman, I pray you, which is the
             way to Master Jew's?

LAUNCELOT   Turn up on your right hand at the next turning,
             but at the next turning of all on your left; marry,   40
             at the very next turning turn of no hand, but turn
             down indirectly to the Jew's house.

GOBBO   By God's sonties, 't will be a hard way to hit. Can
             you tell me whether one Launcelot that dwells with
             him, dwell with him or no?   45

LAUNCELOT   Talk you of young *Master* Launcelot? (*Aside*) Mark
             me now, now will I raise the waters. (*To* GOBBO)
             Talk you of young *Master* Launcelot?

GOBBO   No "master", sir, but a poor man's son. His father,

2.2 Near Shylock's house

Launcelot finally convinces old Gobbo that he is indeed talking to his son; and he tells the old man that he is planning to leave Shylock, and become Bassanio's servant instead.

Activities

Actors' interpretations: visual humour

This edition of the play adds some stage directions to lines 71–106, to help you visualise the action (for example when Launcelot kneels, line 76).

A In pairs, pick out the visual joke which you found funniest and freeze-frame it.

B Imagine you were filming the play. Sketch out three or four frames of a storyboard to show the moments of visual humour.

C Act out lines 71–107, following the stage directions in the text, trying to make the sequence as funny as possible. Then try to think up some different actions for each of those comic moments. (For example, in the 1999 production, Launcelot was carrying a mop – and it was this that Old Gobbo touched on line 91; sometimes Launcelot is overweight, which offers different possibilities for lines 104–107.) Talk about your decisions. Which actions best fit your interpretation of Launcelot?

92 **what a beard...!** *This moment might be a comic parallel of the Jacob story (see 1.3.67–89 and pages 202–203).*

94 **fill-horse** cart-horse

95–96 **grows backward** *gets shorter rather than longer*

99 **agree** get on together

101 **set up my rest** made up my mind (and risked all I have)

104 **halter** hangman's noose

109 **rare new liveries** marvellous new servants' uniforms

112 **I am a Jew if...** *an example of 'Jew' used to mean 'villain' (compare* **a very Jew***, line 103, above)*

114–115 **so hasted** hurried up

115 **farthest** latest

Launcelot my boy.

LAUNCELOT   Pray you, let's have no more fooling about it, but give me your blessing; I am Launcelot your boy that was, your son that is, your child that shall be.

GOBBO   I cannot think you are my son.   85

LAUNCELOT   I know not what I shall think of that; but I am Launcelot, the Jew's man, and I am sure Margery your wife is my mother.

GOBBO   Her name is Margery indeed; I'll be sworn, if thou be Launcelot, thou art mine own flesh and blood.   90 (*He feels the back of* LAUNCELOT'S *head*) Lord! (worshipped might He be), what a beard hast thou got! Thou hast got more hair on thy chin than Dobbin my fill-horse has on his tail.

LAUNCELOT   It should seem, then, that Dobbin's tail grows   95 backward. I am sure he had more hair of his tail than I have of my face, when I last saw him.

GOBBO   Lord, how art thou changed! How dost thou and thy master agree? I have brought him a present; how 'gree you now?   100

LAUNCELOT   Well, well; but for mine own part, as I have set up my rest to run away, so I will not rest till I have run some ground; my master's a very Jew. Give him a present? give him a halter! I am famished in his service (*He makes* GOBBO *feel the fingers of his left*   105 *hand, which he stretches out on his chest like ribs*) You may tell every finger I have with my ribs. Father, I am glad you are come; give me your present to one Master Bassanio, who indeed gives rare new liveries; if I serve not him, I will run as far as God   110 has any ground. O rare fortune! here comes the man; to him father, for I am a Jew if I serve the Jew any longer.

Enter BASSANIO *with* LEONARDO *and a follower or two.*

BASSANIO   (*To one of the men*) You may do so, but let it be so hasted that supper be ready at the farthest by five   115

2.2 Near Shylock's house

After some confusing explanations from Launcelot and his father, Bassanio is made to understand that Launcelot wants to become his servant.

Activities

Shakespeare's language: malapropisms (1)

Like several of Shakespeare's characters, Launcelot and his father are famous for mixing up their words and coming up with some amusing malapropisms. Find the following slips and complete the chart, explaining in each case (a) what the correct word was – the one that the character ought to have been using; (b) what meaning he was trying to get across; and (c) what the actual, mistaken, meaning was:

	(a)	(b)	(c)
	correct word	intended meaning	actual meaning
infection			
frutify			
impertinent			
defect			

How do each of the *actual* meanings add to the humour of the scene? For example, how might Bassanio react when Old Gobbo says that his son has a great infection?

116–117 **put...to making** order the uniforms to be made

118 **anon** immediately

121 **Gramercy** thank you ('God grant mercy')

wouldst thou...me? do you want anything?

125 **infection** *Old Gobbo now starts using malapropisms: he means 'affection' (desire).*

130 **scarce cater-cousins** not exactly the best of friends

133 **fruitify** *He possibly means 'notify' or 'certify'.*

137 **impertinent to** *He means 'pertinent to' (to do with).*

143 **defect** *He means 'effect' (the heart of the matter).*

of the clock. See these letters delivered, put the
liveries to making, and desire Gratiano to come
anon to my lodging.

Exit the man.

LAUNCELOT	To him, father.	
GOBBO	(*To* BASSANIO) God bless your worship.	120
BASSANIO	Gramercy, wouldst thou aught with me?	
GOBBO	Here's my son, sir, a poor boy –	
LAUNCELOT	Not a poor boy, sir, but the rich Jew's man that would, sir – as my father shall specify –	
GOBBO	He hath a great infection, sir, (as one would say) to serve –	125
LAUNCELOT	Indeed, the short and the long is, I serve the Jew, and have a desire – as many father shall specify –	
GOBBO	His master and he (saving your worship's reverence) are scarce cater-cousins, –	130
LAUNCELOT	To be brief, the very truth is that the Jew, having done me wrong, doth cause me – as my father (being, I hope, an old man) shall frutify unto you –	
GOBBO	I have here a dish of doves that I would bestow upon your worship, and my suit is –	135
LAUNCELOT	In very brief, the suit is impertinent to myself, as your worship shall know by this honest old man – and though I say it, though old man, yet, poor man, my father.	140
BASSANIO	One speak for both! – What would you?	
LAUNCELOT	Serve you, sir.	
GOBBO	That is the very defect of the matter, sir.	
BASSANIO	I know thee well; thou hast obtained thy suit,	

2.2 Near Shylock's house

Bassanio agrees to take Launcelot on as a servant – he has already discussed the matter with Shylock – and Launcelot celebrates his good fortune.

Activities

Character review: Launcelot Gobbo (2)

Fortune-telling
Launcelot is so delighted at getting work with Bassanio that he reads his own palm and predicts an outrageously adventurous future (lines 156–168). Redraft his fortune as though it were an entry under 'Your Stars' in *The Rialto* newspaper.

What does this palm-reading speech reveal about the kind of person Launcelot is?

Launcelot Gobbo (Andrew French) (RNT 1999)

---

146 **preferred** recommended

149–151 **old proverb** *The Bible says that God's* **grace** *is* **enough** *for anybody.*

153–154 **inquire...out** find out where I live

155 **guarded** ornamented

156 **I cannot...service, no!** so who was it said I couldn't get a good job?

158 **fairer table** luckier-looking lines on my palm (*for fortune-telling*)

160–161 **simple...life** a life line (*on his palm*) with nothing remarkable about it

161 **small trifle** just a few

163 **coming-in** (1) income; (2) *a sexual innuendo (come)*

163–164 **scape...thrice** escape drowning three times

164–165 **in peril...feather-bed** *This seems to refer to some kind of danger incurred by his (forecasted) active sex-life.*

165 **scapes** escapes (*from tricky sexual situations*)

167 **for this gear** for having given me all this

168 **in the twinkling** *'...of an eye'*: very quickly

170 **orderly bestowed** neatly stowed (*on board ship*)

172 **best-esteemed acquaintance** closest friend

173 **My best...herein** I will get this done as well as I can

Shylock thy master spoke with me this day,   145
And hath preferred thee, if it *be* preferment
To leave a rich Jew's service, to become
The follower of so poor a gentlemen.

LAUNCELOT   The old proverb is very well parted between my
master Shylock and you, sir; you have "the grace of 150
God", sir, and he hath "enough".

BASSANIO   Thou speak'st it well; (*To* GOBBO) go, father, with
thy son –
(*To* LAUNCELOT) Take leave of thy old master, and
inquire
My lodging out. (*To his followers*) Give him a livery
More guarded than his fellows', see it done.   155

LAUNCELOT   Father, in. I cannot get a service, no! I have ne'er
a tongue in my head. (*He looks at the palm of his
hand*) Well, if any man in Italy have a fairer table
which doth offer to swear upon a book, I shall
have good fortune! Go to, here's a simple line of   160
life, here's a small trifle of wives; alas! fifteen wives
is nothing, eleven widows and nine maids is a
simple coming-in for one man, and then to scape
drowning thrice, and to be in peril of my life with
the edge of a feather-bed, here are simple scapes.   165
Well, if Fortune be a woman, she's a good wench
for this gear. Father, come; I'll take my leave of the
Jew in the twinkling.

Exit with old GOBBO.

BASSANIO   I pray thee, good Leonardo, think on this;
These things being bought and orderly bestowed,   170
Return in haste, for I do feast to-night
My best-esteemed acquaintance. Hie thee, go!

LEONARDO   My best endeavours shall be done herein.

He begins to leave.

Enter GRATIANO.

GRATIANO   Where's your master?

2.4 Venice

As Lorenzo and his friends are making plans for a masque that night, Launcelot arrives with the letter from Jessica, and explains that he is off to invite Shylock to dinner with Bassanio.

Activities

Plot review (3): the masque

Lorenzo and the others plan to spirit Jessica away under the cover of a masque. List the reasons why this would be an ideal circumstance for her escape. Read the whole of 2.4 and improvise a conversation in which Gratiano meets up with Salerio and explains exactly what the plan is. Explain:

- when and where you will all meet up
- what Jessica plans to do before escaping
- why she will not be recognised or noticed out in the street
- where Shylock will be during Jessica's escape.

There are important clues about their plot in:

- line 1 (why should they have to 'slink away' from supper?)
- lines 17–18 (why is this important to their plans?).

1 **slink** sneak, slip

5 **spoke us** discussed arrangements about

torch-bearers *Masques (parties in which people disguised themselves) were often torch-lit.*

6 **'Tis vile...ordered** it will be rubbish if it isn't cleverly planned

9 **furnish us** get everything we need

10–11 **An it...signify** if you would like to open the seal on this letter, you'll find out what it means

12 **hand** handwriting

15 **By your leave** If you'll excuse me...

23 **of** with (*Jessica, disguised as a page, will be his torch-bearer; see lines 33 and 40*)

Scene 4

Venice. A street.

Enter GRATIANO, LORENZO, SALERIO *and* SOLANIO.

LORENZO Nay, we will slink away in supper-time,
Disguise us at my lodging, and return
All in an hour.

GRATIANO We have not made good preparation.

SALERIO We have not spoke us yet of torch-bearers. 5

SOLANIO 'T is vile unless it may be quaintly ordered,
And better in my mind not undertook.

LORENZO 'T is now but four of clock; we have two hours
To furnish us –

Enter LAUNCELOT, *with a letter.*

       friend Launcelot, what's the news?

LAUNCELOT An it shall please you to break up this, it shall seem 10
to signify.

LORENZO I know the hand; in faith, 't is a fair hand,
And whiter than the paper it writ on
Is the fair hand that writ.

GRATIANO   Love-news, in faith.

LAUNCELOT By your leave, sir. 15

LORENZO Whither goest thou?

LAUNCELOT Marry, sir, to bid my old master the Jew to sup
to-night with my new master the Christian.

LORENZO Hold here, take this; (He *gives* LAUNCELOT *some*
money) tell gentle Jessica
I will not fail her; speak it privately, (*Exit* LAUNCELOT) 20
Go, gentlemen,
Will you prepare you for this masque to-night?
I am provided of a torch-bearer.

2.5 Venice: Shylock's house

Shylock has been invited to dine with Antonio and Bassanio, but he is uneasy about it and reluctant to leave the house; when he hears about the masque, he sternly orders Jessica to shut all the doors and keep away from the windows.

Activities

Character review: Shylock (5)

Shylock has accepted the Christians' invitation to supper, despite having told them earlier that he would not dine with them (1.3.31–35). Why do you think he might have changed his mind? Improvise a conversation between Shylock and a friend (perhaps Tubal, who is referred to at 1.3.54 and appears in 3.1), in which Shylock explains his thinking about the supper invitation.

Shakespeare's language: malapropisms (2)

Remind yourself about Launcelot's malapropisms by looking back at the activity on page 44. Can you explain the joke in the exchange between Launcelot and Shylock on lines 19–21?

8 **was wont to** always used to

9 **without bidding** without being asked

11 **bid forth** invited out

14–15 **to feed...Christian** to eat at the wasteful (**prodigal**) Christian's expense

16 **Look to** take good care of

right loath very reluctant

17 **some ill...rest** some trouble brewing which will upset me

18 **dream of money-bags** *thought to be bad luck*

to-night last night

19 **beseech** beg

20 **reproach** *He means 'approach'.*

21 **So do I his** I expect his reproach (= *criticism*)

22 **conspired** plotted

24–27 **my nose fell a-bleeding...** *a mockery of fortune-telling by omens; perhaps Launcelot is playing upon Shylock's superstitions (see lines 17–18)*

30 **wry-necked fife** flute (*played with the musician's neck twisted sideways*)

31 **Clamber not...casements** don't climb up to the windows

33 **varnished** *because they are wearing masks*

35 **fopp'ry** foolishness, stupidity

37 **no mind of feasting forth** no wish to go out to eat

LAUNCELOT   Your worship was wont to tell me I could do
              nothing without bidding.

Enter JESSICA.

JESSICA   Call you? what is your will?   10

SHYLOCK   I am bid forth to supper, Jessica;
              There are my keys – but wherefore should I go?
              I am not bid for love; they flatter me;
              But yet I'll go in hate, to feed upon
              The prodigal Christian. Jessica, my girl,   15
              Look to my house. I am right loath to go;
              There is some ill a-brewing towards my rest,
              For I did dream of money-bags to-night.

LAUNCELOT   I beseech you, sir, go; my young master doth
              expect your reproach.   20

SHYLOCK   So do I his.

LAUNCELOT   And they have conspired together; I will not say
              you shall see a masque, but if you do, then it was
              not for nothing that my nose fell a-bleeding on
              Black-Monday last, at six o'clock i' th' morning,   25
              falling out that year on Ash-Wednesday was four
              year in th' afternoon.

SHYLOCK   What, are there masques? Hear you me, Jessica,
              Lock up my doors, and when you hear the drum,
              And the vile squealing of the wry-necked fife,   30
              Clamber not you up to the casements then,
              Nor thrust your head into the public street
              To gaze on Christian fools with varnished faces;
              But stop my house's ears – I mean my casements –
              Let not the sound of shallow fopp'ry enter   35
              My sober house. By Jacob's staff I swear
              I have no mind of feasting forth to-night;
              But I will go. (*To* LAUNCELOT) Go you before me, sirrah;
              Say I will come.

LAUNCELOT   I will go before, sir.
              (*To* JESSICA) Mistress, look out at window, for all this – 40

2.6 Outside Shylock's house

Launcelot secretly tells Jessica to watch out for Lorenzo. Then, as Shylock leaves, still full of misgivings, his daughter plans her escape. Later that evening, Gratiano and Salerio wait outside Shylock's house, where they have arranged to meet Lorenzo.

Activities

Character review: Shylock (6)

Father and daughter

Philip Voss (Shylock in 1997) said: 'The way I play it, he does love her...I think Jessica just rebels. I don't know how my constraints are affecting her: I'm doing it for her own Jewish good. But I hope we've found a way of showing, even in a short scene, the complex and loving relationship that we have.'

Do you feel that Shylock genuinely loves his daughter? What kind of love is it? And does she love him in return?

In groups of three, act out the scene to bring out the fact that Shylock and Jessica actually do love each other. (In many productions, Shylock strokes his daughter's hair, for example, or she helps him on with his coat.)

How do you feel at the end of the scene about (a) Shylock, and (b) Jessica, if it is done in this way?

---

42 **worth a Jewess' eye** worth a great deal of money

45 **patch** fool (*professional fools wore patched costumes*)

46 **Snail-slow in profit** slow to learn or improve himself

47 **drones hive...me** there is no room in my hive for bees that do no work

50 **borrowed purse** *the money that Bassanio has borrowed from Antonio*

53 **"Fast bind, fast find"** lock up securely and everything will be safe when you return

54 **never stale** never out of fashion; always relevant

in thrifty mind to a person careful with their possessions

55 **crost** prevented by bad luck

1 **penthouse** porch with a sloping roof

2 **desired...stand** wanted us to wait

3–4 **it is a marvel...clock** it's amazing that he's late: lovers are usually early

5–7 **O ten...unforfeited** people who have only just fallen in love are much more eager to keep their promises to each other than they are once they are married

Venus' pigeons *the doves which draw the chariot of the goddess of love*

There will come a Christian by
Will be worth a Jewess' eye.

Exit.

SHYLOCK   What says that fool of Hagar's offspring? ha?

JESSICA   His words were, "Farewell, mistress"; nothing else.

SHYLOCK   The patch is kind enough, but a huge feeder,   45
Snail-slow in profit, and he sleeps by day
More than the wild-cat; drones hive not with me,
Therefore I part with him, and part with him
To one that I would have him help to waste
His borrowed purse. Well, Jessica, go in –   50
Perhaps I will return immediately –
Do as I bid you; shut doors after you –
"Fast bind, fast find" –
A proverb never stale in thrifty mind.

Exit.

JESSICA   Farewell; and if my fortune be not crost,   55
I have a father, you a daughter, lost

Exit.

Scene 6

Venice. Outside Shylock's house.

Enter GRATIANO *and* SALERIO, *dressed for the masque.*

GRATIANO   This is the penthouse under which Lorenzo
Desired us to make stand.

SALERIO   His hour is almost past.

GRATIANO   And it is marvel he out-dwells his hour,
For lovers ever run before the clock.

SALERIO   O ten times faster Venus' pigeons fly   5
To seal love's bonds new-made, than they are wont
To keep obligèd faith unforfeited!

2.6 Outside Shylock's house

Lorenzo arrives at last and calls out to Jessica, who throws a casket full of jewels down to her lover.

Activities

Shakespeare's language: imagery

Check that you understand Gratiano's 'All things ... enjoyed' (lines 12–13).

A What does he mean? How do the examples of eating (lines 8–9) and horses (lines 10–12) help his argument? Think of examples from your own lives which support his point.

B Gratiano seems to weave together two images in lines 14–19: a ship setting sail; and a young man leaving home. Draw a series of cartoon frames to illustrate these two interweaving images.

C Why do you think Shakespeare included this speech here? Talk about the following possible reasons:
- The central point (lines 12–13) has a significance for other parts of the play.
- The images of 'the prodigal' (lines 14–19) remind us about Bassanio's wastefulness with money.
- Shakespeare is giving Jessica time to get changed into boys' clothes.
- The whole conversation (lines 1–19) helps to give the impression that time has passed during which Shylock has been to supper with Antonio.

8 **That ever holds** that's always the case

10–12 **Where is...first?** where do you find a horse which is as eager to retrace his steps as he was to set out?

12–13 **All things...enjoyed** It's more fun looking forward to something than actually achieving it.

14–16 **How like...wind!** a ship decorated with flags (**scarfèd**) sets out from her home harbour like a younger son or a spendthrift (**prodigal**), being hugged and kissed by a prostitute (**strumpet**) who is after his money

18 **over-weathered ribs** *ship's hull damaged by the sea and bad weather*

19 **rent** torn

20 **hereafter** later

21 **your patience...abode** I apologise for being late

23 **you shall please** you want

25 **father** *he will soon be Lorenzo's father-in-law*

s.d. **above** *on the balcony (see pages 197–199)*

27 **Albeit** although

33 **pains** trouble

35 **exchange** disguise

GRATIANO	That ever holds; who riseth from a feast
	With that keen appetite that he sits down?
	Where is the horse that doth untread again	10
	His tedious measures with the unbated fire
	That he did pace them first? All things that are,
	Are with more spirit chasèd than enjoyed.
	How like a younger or a prodigal
	The scarfèd bark puts from her native bay,	15
	Hugged and embracèd by the strumpet wind!
	How like the prodigal doth she return
	With over-weathered ribs and ragged sails,
	Lean, rent, and beggared by the strumpet wind!

Enter LORENZO.

| SALERIO | Here comes Lorenzo; more of this hereafter. | 20 |

LORENZO	Sweet friends, your patience for my long abode;
	Not I but my affairs have made you wait;
	When you shall please to play the thieves for wives,
	I'll watch as long for you then. Approach –
	Here dwells my father Jew. Ho! who's
	within?	25

Enter JESSICA above, in boy's clothes.

| JESSICA | Who are you? Tell me, for more certainty – |
| | Albeit I'll swear that I do know your tongue. |

| LORENZO | Lorenzo and thy love. |

JESSICA	Lorenzo, certain, and my love indeed;
	For who love I so much? and now who
	knows	30
	But you Lorenzo whether I am yours?

| LORENZO | Heaven and thy thoughts are witness that thou art. |

JESSICA	(*Throwing down a box*)
	Here, catch this casket; it is worth the pains.
	I am glad 't is night – you do not look on me –
	For I am much ashamed of my exchange;	35
	But love is blind, and lovers cannot see
	The pretty follies that themselves commit,
	For if they could, Cupid himself would blush

2.6 Outside Shylock's house

Jessica is embarrassed to be disguised as a boy, but agrees to join Lorenzo –
after she has taken more of Shylock's jewels and gold. As they run away
together, Antonio arrives in some haste.

Activities

Actors' interpretations: boy actors

In Shakespeare's time, Jessica would
have been played by a boy actor (as
would all young female characters in the
theatre). What difference would that have
made to the audience's reaction to lines
34–45? Is it odd to hear Lorenzo talking
to a boy actor about 'the lovely garnish of
a boy'?

**Actors' interpretations: using the
balcony**

Look at pages 197–199 to see the design
of Shakespeare's stage. Jessica would
almost certainly have appeared on the
stage balcony for her exchange with
Lorenzo (lines 26–50).
1. Draw your impression of what the
   scene might look like.
2. How does Shakespeare give Jessica
   time to get down on to the main
   stage?

41 **hold a candle...** stand by and
observe my shameful
appearance

42 **light** *There is a pun here: light
could also mean sexually
immodest (compare 5.1.129).*

43–44 **'tis an office...obscured** the
light would serve to show me
up and I ought to remain hidden

44–45 **So you are...boy** you are
'obscured' – by your lovely
disguise as a boy

47 **For the close...runaway** the
secretive night is passing
quickly

48 **stayed for** waited for

49 **gild myself** cover myself with
gold (**more ducats**)

51 **by my hood** *No one is really
sure what this means; perhaps
he is swearing by the hood of
his disguise.*

gentle (1) gentile; (2) kind
person (*the same pun as 1.3.174
and 2.4.35*)

52 **Beshrew** curse ('damn me')

59 **Our masquing...stay** our other
friends at the party must by
now be waiting for us

62 **Fie, fie** an expression of
impatience (*compare 1.1.46*)

63 **stay** are waiting

64 **is come about** is now blowing
in the right direction (*the ship
can sail*)

To see me thus transformèd to a boy.

LORENZO Descend, for you must be my torch-bearer.   40

JESSICA What, must I hold a candle to my shames?
They in themselves, good sooth, are too too light.
Why, 't is an office of discovery, love,
And I should be obscured.

LORENZO   So are you, sweet,
Even in the lovely garnish of a boy.   45
But come at once,
For the close night doth play the runaway,
And we are stayed for at Bassanio's feast.

JESSICA I will make fast the doors, and gild myself
With some more ducats, and be with you
        straight.   50

                                                            Exit.

GRATIANO Now, by my hood, a gentle and no Jew.

LORENZO Beshrew me but I love her heartily;
For she is wise, if I can judge of her;
And fair she is, if that mine eyes be true;
And true she is, as she hath proved herself: 55
And therefore like herself, wise, fair, and true,
Shall she be placèd in my constant soul.

Enter JESSICA, *below.*

(*To* JESSICA) What, art thou come? On, gentlemen,
        away!
Our masquing mates by this time for us stay.

Exit with JESSICA *and* SALERIO; GRATIANO *is about to follow them. Enter*
ANTONIO.

ANTONIO Who's there?   60

GRATIANO Signior Antonio?

ANTONIO Fie, fie, Gratiano! where are all the rest?
'T is nine o'clock; our friends all stay for you.
No masque to-night – the wind is come about;

2.7 Belmont: Portia's house

Antonio tells Gratiano that he has no time to take part in the masque: the wind has changed and Bassanio's ship is ready to set sail. In Belmont, Morocco begins his choice of the caskets and reads their inscriptions.

Activities

Character review: Antonio (3)

Does he know about the plot?
Antonio's servants have been all over Venice looking for Lorenzo and the others: the masque is cancelled as they have to board ship. Does this mean that Antonio has no idea of the plan by Lorenzo and the others to spirit Jessica away while Shylock was dining with him? Why might they have decided not to tell him?

Plot review (4): the caskets

Start to design a poster in the form of a triptych (three pictures, side-by-side, on the same theme): the left-hand panel will be devoted to gold, the centre lead and the right silver. Each panel will have:
- a picture of the casket (your own design)
- the inscription on the outside
- something to represent the suitor who chooses that casket
- the object inside it
- the writing on the scroll inside
- the 'message' of the scroll, in your own words.

67 **on't** of it

s.d. **flourish of cornets** trumpets are blown

    trains groups of attendants

1 **discover** reveal

2 **several** different, various

8 **dull** not shiny

    as blunt as outspoken and direct (*dull could also mean blunt, when used of a sword*)

9 **hazard** risk, gamble

12 **withal** with it, as well

14 **back again** over again

19 **fair advantages** a good profit

20 **shows of dross** promises of rubbish

21 **I'll then…aught** I will therefore neither give nor risk anything

Bassanio presently will go aboard;   65
I have sent twenty out to seek for you.

GRATIANO   I am glad on 't; I desire no more delight
Than to be under sail, and gone to-night.

Exeunt.

Scene 7

Belmont. A room in Portia's house.

Flourish of cornets. Enter PORTIA *with* MOROCCO *and both their trains.*

PORTIA   (*To her attendants*)
Go, draw aside the curtains and discover
The several caskets to this noble prince.
(*To* MOROCCO) Now make your choice.

MOROCCO   This first of gold, who this inscription bears:
"Who chooseth me shall gain what many men
    desire."   5
The second silver, which this promise carries:
"Who chooseth me shall get as much as he
    deserves."
This third, dull lead, with warning all as blunt,
"Who chooseth me must give and hazard all he
    hath."
How shall I know if I do choose the right?   10

PORTIA   The one of them contains my picture, prince;
If you choose that, then I am yours withal.

MOROCCO   Some god direct my judgement! let me see,
I will survey th' inscriptions back again.
What says this leaden casket?   15
"Who chooseth me must give and hazard all he
    hath."
Must give – for what? for lead, hazard for lead!
This casket threatens – men that hazard all
Do it in hope of fair advantages;
A golden mind stoops not to shows of dross,   20
I'll then nor give nor hazard aught for lead.

2.7 Belmont: Portia's house

Morocco gives his reasons for rejecting the lead and the silver caskets, and chooses gold because it is the only metal fine enough to contain Portia's picture.

22 **virgin hue** pure colour (*silver was also associated with Diana, goddess of young women, see 1.2.103*)

25 **even** fair

26 **be'st rated by thy estimation** are judged on your reputation

29–30 **to be afeard...myself** to doubt that I deserve her would be to belittle myself

32–34 **I do...breeding** *He is as noble and as wealthy as Portia.*

36 **graved** engraved

40–41 **shrine...saint** *Morocco sees the quest for Portia as a religious pilgrimage to a living (*mortal breathing*) saint.*

41 **Hyrcanian** *These deserts, south of the Caspian Sea, were famous for their savage animals and barrenness.*

vasty wilds immense wilderness

42 **as thoroughfares** like roads

44–46 **The watery...spirits** the sea, whose wave-tops attempt to spit at the sky, is no barrier to the courageous travellers from abroad

47 **As o'er a brook** as if crossing a stream

50 **base** low and unworthy (*with a pun on the 'base' metal, lead*)

50–51 **it were...grave** it would be too gross to think that her burial sheet could be enclosed in a dark grave (**cerecloth:** *corpses were wrapped in a waxed cloth*)

52 **immured** walled in; shut away

53 **ten times** *Gold at that time was ten times more valuable than silver.*

tried tried and tested; dependable

55–56 **They have...angel** *There was a gold coin in use in Shakespeare's time called an 'angel' because it bore the picture of the archangel Michael.*

57 **insculped upon** engraved on the surface (*in contrast to the 'angel' who lies within [line 59] the right casket*)

60 **thrive I as I may!** may I succeed!

61 **form** picture

Portia (Derbhla Crotty) holding the hand of Morocco (Chu Omambala) (RNT 1999)

What says the silver with her virgin hue?
"Who chooseth me shall get as much as he deserves."
As much as he deserves! Pause there, Morocco,
And weigh thy value with an even hand.   25
If thou be'st rated by thy estimation,
Thou dost deserve enough; and yet enough
May not extend so far as to the lady;
And yet to be afeard of my deserving
Were but a weak disabling of myself.   30
As much as I deserve – why, that's the lady!
I do in birth deserve her, and in fortunes,
In graces, and in qualities of breeding;
But more than these, in love I do deserve –
What if I strayed no further, but chose here?   35
Let's see once more this saying graved in gold:
"Who chooseth me shall gain what many men
        desire."
Why, that's the lady – all the world desires her.
From the four corners of the earth they come
To kiss this shrine, this mortal breathing
        saint.   40
The Hyrcanian deserts, and the vasty wilds
Of wide Arabia are as throughfares now
For princes to come view fair Portia.
The watery kingdom, whose ambitious head
Spits in the face of heaven, is no bar   45
To stop the foreign spirits, but they come
As o'er brook to see fair Portia.
One of these three contains her heavenly picture.
Is't like that lead contains her? 'T were damnation
To think so base a thought; it were too gross   50
To rib her cerecloth in the obscure grave;
Or shall I think in silver she's immured,
Being ten times undervalued to tried gold?
O sinful thought! never so rich a gem
Was set in worse than gold. They have in England   55
A coin that bears the figure of an angel
Stamped in gold, but that's insculped upon;
But here an angel in a golden bed
Lies all within. Deliver me the key;
Here do I choose, and thrive I as I may!   60

PORTIA   There, take it, prince, and if my form lie there,

2.8 Venice

Morocco opens the gold casket. Finding that it contains a skull with a scroll through its eye, he reads the message and leaves. Back in Venice, Salerio and Solanio talk about the outcry following Jessica's elopement: Shylock has enlisted the help of the Duke in his search for Lorenzo and his daughter.

Activities

Plot review (5): the caskets

Add to your plan for a triptych, by noting down the contents of the gold casket. You can now plan a sketch of that panel.

Shakespeare's language: is Portia racist?

Many people in Shakespeare's time believed that the body contained four 'humours' – fluids which controlled our behaviour and personality. Every individual had a different mixture (or *complexion*) of these humours. If you had too much of a particular humour, it would show in your face, which is how we get the modern meaning of the word 'complexion'.

1. Is Portia's final line a reference to Morocco's personality or his skin colour?
2. Is Portia racist?
3. If you were directing the play, how would you answer the actress playing Portia, if she asked for the line be cut in performance, so as not to cause offence? (She explains that, even if you decide that 'complexion' has its older meaning here, most people in the audience will still assume it is a reference to Morocco's colour.)

63 **carrion Death** skull

65 **glisters** glitters (*a well-known proverb*)

68 **my outside** *the gold of which the casket is made*

71 **Young in limbs...old** young in body but mature in judgement

72 **inscrolled** written on this scroll

73 **your suit is cold** you have failed in your wooing

77 **To take...part** to boringly stretch out my leave-taking; this is how losers depart

78 **gentle riddance** *she has got rid of him, but politely*

79 **of his complexion** (1) of his temperament, personality or character; (2) of his skin colour (*see the activity on the left*)

1–3 **under sail** *Bassanio and Gratiano have set sail for Belmont, but Lorenzo and Jessica have taken a different route (see lines 7–10).*

4 **raised** roused up

2.8

Then I am yours!

He unlocks the golden casket.

MOROCCO   O hell! what have we here?
A carrion Death, within whose empty eye
There is a written scroll – I'll read the writing.
All that glisters is not gold;   65
Often have you heard that told.
Many a man his life hath sold
But my outside to behold.
Gilded tombs do worms infold;
Had you been as wise as bold,   70
Young in limbs, in judgement old,
Your answer had not been inscrolled.
Fare you well; your suit is cold.
Cold indeed and labour lost;
Then, farewell, heat, and welcome, frost!   75
Portia, adieu! I have too grieved a heart
To take a tedious leave; thus losers part.

Exit with his train.

PORTIA   A gentle riddance. (*To her attendants*) Draw the
         curtains; go.
Let all of his complexion choose me so.

Exeunt.

Scene 8

Venice. A street.

Enter SALERIO *and* SOLANIO.

SALERIO   Why, man, I saw Bassanio under sail;
With him is Gratiano gone along,
And in their ship I am sure Lorenzo is not.

SOLANIO   The villain Jew with outcries raised the Duke,
Who went with him to search Bassanio's
         ship.   5

SALERIO   He came too late; the ship was under sail;

2.8 Venice

Salerio and Solanio describe Shylock's frenzied reaction to his daughter's flight. They express their concerns about Antonio: he had better repay the loan on time – Shylock is bitter about his daughter's elopement with a Christian.

Activities

Character review: Shylock (7):

'O my ducats! O my daughter!'
In most productions, Salerio and Solanio report Shylock's behaviour with great amusement (lines 12–24). Act out the dialogue in that way, so as to mock Shylock's ranting.

- How do they get the maximum of humour and mockery into their account? Look at Solanio's language.
- How accurate is their report, do you think? Did Shylock really behave in this way, or are they exaggerating because they hate him? Find evidence which suggests that they are anti-Semitic (see pages 200–201).
- Look at the description again. Is it possible to feel sympathy for Shylock at this point? What do you think his real values are?

8 **gondola** *boat used as a Venetian taxi service on the canals*

9 **amorous** loving

12 **a passion so confused** such a mixture of passionate outbursts

13 **variable** constantly changing

16 **Christian ducats** *either* (1) ducats gained in interest from Christians; *or* (2) ducats now in Christian hands

19 **double ducats** *coins worth double an ordinary ducat*

20 **stones** gem stones (*but this is also a bawdy pun: 'stones' are testicles*)

25 **look he...day** takes good care to meet the deadline (*for repaying the money*)

27 **reasoned** talked

28 **narrow seas...** the English Channel

29–30 **there miscarried A vessel** a ship was wrecked

30 **richly fraught** laden with riches; carrying valuable cargo

37–38 **make some...return** get back as quickly as he could

39 **Slubber not business** don't carry out your business carelessly

40 **stay...time** wait until the time is right to complete your business properly

42 **mind of** mind preoccupied with

But there the Duke was given to understand
That in a gondola were seen together
Lorenzo and his amorous Jessica.
Besides, Antonio certified the Duke   10
They were not with Bassanio in his ship.

SOLANIO   I never heard a passion so confused,
So strange, outrageous, and so variable,
As the dog Jew did utter in the streets:
"My daughter! O my ducats! O my daughter!   15
Fled with a Christian! O my Christian ducats!
Justice, the law, my ducats, and my daughter!
A sealèd bag, two sealèd bags of ducats,
Of double ducats, stolen from me by my daughter!
And jewels, two stones, two rich and precious
     stones,   20
Stolen by my daughter! Justice! find the girl!
She hath the stones upon her, and the ducats!"

SALERIO   Why all the boys in Venice follow him,
Crying, his stones, his daughter, and his ducats.

SOLANIO   Let good Antonio look he keep his day   25
Or he shall pay for this.

SALERIO   Marry, well remembered.
I reasoned with a Frenchman yesterday,
Who told me, in the narrow seas that part
The French and English, there miscarried
A vessel of our country, richly fraught;   30
I thought upon Antonio when he told me,
And wished in silence that it were not his.

SOLANIO   You were best to tell Antonio what you hear;
Yet do not suddenly, for it may grieve him.

SALERIO   A kinder gentleman treads not the earth;   35
I saw Bassanio and Antonio part;
Bassanio told him he would make some speed
Of his return. He answered, "Do not so;
Slubber not business for my sake, Bassanio,
But stay the very riping of the time,   40
And for the Jew's bond which he hath of me,
Let it not enter in your mind of love.

2.9 Belmont: Portia's house

Arragon rejects lead and gold, but his eye is caught by the silver casket and its inscription.

Activities

Actors' interpretations: Morocco and Arragon

Like Morocco, Arragon is often portrayed as an extremely comic character. How could this scene be made comic? Think about the different ways in which Arragon could be performed, for example: in one production, he was extremely old; often he speaks in a very strong Spanish accent.

Talk together about why Morocco would make (a) a good husband; and (b) a bad one, for Portia. Then do the same with Arragon.

Themes: appearance and reality (3)

Re-read:
• Morocco's thoughts (2.7.48–59)
• the scroll in the gold casket (2.7.65–69)
• Arragon's words (2.9.25–30 and 37–49).

What do each of those add to the theme of appearance and reality?

Look back at the activity on page 48 and make further plans for your wall-chart.

17 **injunctions** commands

19 **addressed me** prepared myself

25–26 **that "many"…show** that word 'many' might mean the stupid majority of people who judge by outward appearances

28 **pries not to th' interior** does not look into the inside

martlet house martin

30 **Even in…casualty** even where accidents are most likely to strike, and with most force

32 **jump…spirits** agree with ordinary people

38 **cozen** cheat

39–40 **be honourable…merit** claim to be honourable without any evidence of the fact

41 **estates, degrees and offices** property, rank and positions

43 **purchased by…wearer** earned only by people who deserve it

44 **How many…bare!** a lot of people who now have to remove their hats in the presence of their 'betters' (**stand bare**) would keep them on (**cover**)!

46–49 **How much low…varnished!** among the people who are currently born nobles (**true seed of honour**), there are many who ought to be picked out (**gleaned**) and rejected as peasants; and many people ruined by these hard times who ought to be newly decorated with honours

PORTIA	To these injunctions every one doth swear	
	That comes to hazard for my worthless self.	
ARRAGON	And so have I addressed me – fortune now	
	To my heart's hope! Gold, silver, and base lead.	20
	"Who chooseth me must give and hazard all he hath."	
	You shall look fairer, ere I give or hazard.	
	What says the golden chest? ha! let me see,	
	"Who chooseth me shall gain what many men desire."	
	What many men desire – that "many" may be meant	25
	By the fool multitude that choose by show,	
	Not learning more than the fond eye doth teach,	
	Which pries not to th' interior, but, like the martlet,	
	Builds in the weather on the outward wall,	
	Even in the force and road of casualty.	30
	I will not choose what many men desire,	
	Because I will not jump with common spirits,	
	And rank me with the barbarous multitudes.	
	Why, then, to thee, thou silver treasure house,	
	Tell me once more what title thou dost bear:	35
	"Who chooseth me shall get as much as he deserves."	
	And well said, too; for who shall go about	
	To cozen Fortune, and be honourable	
	Without the stamp of merit? Let none presume	
	To wear an undeservèd dignity;	40
	O that estates, degrees, and offices,	
	Were not derived corruptly, and that clear honour	
	Were purchased by the merit of the wearer!	
	How many then should cover that stand bare!	
	How many be commanded that command!	45
	How much low peasantry would then be gleaned	
	From the true seed of honour! and how much honour	
	Picked from the chaff and ruin of the times,	
	To be new-varnished! Well, but to my choice.	
	"Who chooseth me shall get as much as he deserves" –	50

Exam practice

Character review: Portia (3)

Her thoughts and feelings
Portia has much to think about after Arragon has made his choice of caskets.

Imagine you are Portia. Write down your thoughts and feelings as you leave the room, having heard that a new suitor is on his way. You could begin: *Thank goodness these two suitors chose the wrong caskets...*

Before you begin to write, you should think about Portia's views on:
- her father's will, and the caskets
- the two recent suitors: Morocco and Arragon
- her hopes about the suitor who is about to arrive.

Actors' interpretations: Venice and Belmont (1)

Some people take the view that Shakespeare draws a number of contrasts between the two locations of Venice and Belmont.
1. Look back through the play and make notes on which main actions take place in which of the two locations.
2. If you were directing the play, what would you do to help the audience to distinguish clearly between the two locations (a) in a film; (b) in a stage production which used scenery; (c) on Shakespeare's Globe stage (see pages 197–199)?

Plot review (7): linking the strands

Shakespeare seems to have got his ideas for the story of *The Merchant of Venice* from several different old tales, which he then wove together into three plot strands.

The three strands involve:
A Antonio, Shylock and the pound of flesh
B Portia, Bassanio and the caskets
C Lorenzo and Jessica.

Copy the chart opposite and add details to the relevant boxes, to show:
(a) what happens to the characters in that scene
(b) how their plot strand is linked to each of the other two strands in that scene.

To start you off, the boxes for Act 1 have been filled in. Complete the details for Act 2 and continue the chart after Acts 3, 4 and 5.

Actors' interpretations: Shylock's return

Since the time of Henry Irving in the nineteenth century, many actors have chosen to add a scene between 2.6 and 2.7, in which we see Shylock returning from his supper with the Christians only to find that his daughter has gone. Act out the following versions of that return:
- Shylock appears crossing a canal bridge, lantern in hand; he knocks on his door, but there is no reply... (Henry Irving, 1879)
- He returns, enters the house, and is heard running from room to room – occasionally seen at the windows – shouting his daughter's name (Herbert Beerbohm Tree, 1908)

- Before he gets home, he stumbles into the masque and is pushed around by the masquers until he suddenly sees his daughter among them, and cries out as she is swept away from him… (Philip Voss, 1997).

Try other versions of your own. Do they cause us to laugh at Shylock, or feel sympathy for him?

Would you add a moment such as this, if you were directing the play?

Plot review (8): the caskets

Look at the scroll activity on page 76 and add details to your planned triptych.

Themes: love (1)

Lorenzo and Jessica
How would you describe the love between Lorenzo and Jessica?
1. Look at what Lorenzo says about her. How does he describe her, for example? What does he say to her when we see them together?
2. What does Jessica say about (a) her plans to marry Lorenzo and (b) her love for him?
3. How would you answer someone who said: 'This isn't a genuine love on either side. They might think they love each other; but, in fact, he only wants her for her father's money; and she is only using him as a means of escape.'?

PLOT CHART		Act 1, scene 1	Act 1, scene 2	Act 1, scene 3
Strand A Antonio, Shylock and the pound of flesh	Action	Antonio is sad. Bassanio tells him about Portia and asks for a loan. Antonio agrees and is prepared to borrow the money that Bassanio needs.		Shylock meets Antonio and Bassanio. Antonio agrees to the bond, including the pound of flesh clause.
	Links with Strand B	Bassanio describes Portia.		Antonio enters the agreement with Shylock only because Bassanio needs money to woo Portia.
	Links with Strand C	Lorenzo has arrived with Bassanio. They agree to meet at dinner time.		We get a first glimpse of Jessica's way of life.
Strand B Portia, Bassanio and the caskets	Action		Portia and Nerissa discuss the terms of the will and talk about the current batch of suitors.	
	Links with Strand A		Portia remembers an earlier visit from Bassanio.	
	Links with Strand C		—	
Strand C Jessica and Lorenzo	Action			
	Links with Strand A			
	Links with Strand B			

3.1 Near Shylock's house

As Salerio and Solanio go off in response to a message from Antonio, Shylock's friend Tubal arrives. He has been on a long journey in search of Jessica, but has been unable to catch up with her.

Activities

Character review: Shylock (9)

'hath not a Jew eyes…?'
Shylock's reply to Salerio and Solanio (lines 49–69) is one of the most famous speeches in all of Shakespeare's plays. But what exactly is Shylock saying? And how does he say it?

A To gain a grasp of the main points of Shylock's speech, copy and complete the following statements in your own words:

- This is what Antonio has done to me in the past: he has (lines 50–54)...........
  ....
- And why has he done these things? Because (line 54)................................
- Physically, Jews are the same as Christians; for example (lines 54–62)....
  ....
- If Jews and Christians are the same physically, you have to expect that we will be the same when it comes to our behaviour, especially (lines 62–67)........
  ....
- I will not only imitate your Christian behaviour, but (lines 67–69).................
  ....

Continued on page 88

66 **what should his sufferance be?** what patient response should he make?

68 **execute** carry out

68 **it shall go hard…instruction** unless I'm prevented, I will go one better than my teachers

73–74 **cannot be matched** cannot be found to match them

75 **Genoa** *an Italian port*

80 **Frankfort** *Frankfurt: a German city, site of a famous jewellery fair*

80–81 **the curse never fell…** *Shylock refers to the curse supposedly laid upon the Jews for their part in Jesus's crucifixion (see pages 200–201).*

83 **would** wish

85 **hearsed** placed in her coffin

90 **lights on** lands upon

Christian wrong a Jew, what should his sufferance
be by Christian example? Why, revenge! The
villainy you teach me I will execute, and it shall go
hard but I will better the instruction.

Enter a SERVING-MAN *from* ANTONIO.

SERVING-MAN	Gentlemen, my master Antonio is at his house, and desires to speak with you both.	70

| SALERIO | We have been up and down to seek him. | |

Enter TUBAL.

| SOLANIO | Here comes another of the tribe; a third cannot be matched unless the devil himself turn Jew. | |

Exeunt SOLANIO *and* SALERIO *with the* SERVING-MAN

| SHYLOCK | How now, Tubal! what news from Genoa? has thou found my daughter? | 75 |

| TUBAL | I often came where I did hear of her, but cannot find her. | |

| SHYLOCK | Why there, there, there, there! A diamond gone cost me two thousand ducats in Frankfort! The curse never fell upon our nation till now – I never felt it till now. Two thousand ducats in that and other precious, precious jewels. I would my daughter were dead at my foot, and the jewels in her ear; would she were hearsed at my foot, and the ducats in her coffin. No news of them? why, so! And I know not what's spent in the search. Why thou – loss upon loss! The thief gone with so much, and so much to find the thief, and no satisfaction, no revenge, nor no ill luck stirring but what lights on *my* shoulders, no sighs but of *my* breathing, no tears but of *my* shedding. | 80

85

90 |

| TUBAL | Yes, other men have ill luck too – Antonio, as I heard in Genoa – | |

| SHYLOCK | What, what, what? ill luck, ill luck? | 95 |

3.2 Belmont: Portia's house

Bassanio has arrived in Belmont. Portia is anxious for him to take time before making his choice, but he is in torment and wants to get it over with.

1 **tarry** wait

2 **hazard** gamble (*by choosing one of the caskets*)

 in choosing if you choose

3 **forbear** wait

5 **would not** do not want

6 **Hate counsels...quality** hatred does not give that sort of advice

8 **a maiden...thought** a modest young woman should keep her thoughts and feelings to herself

10 **venture** take a chance (*compare* **hazard***, line 2*)

11 **then I am forsworn** if I did that, I would be breaking my oath

12 **So will I never be** and I will never do that

14 **Beshrew** damn (*but a milder oath in Shakespeare's time*)

15 **o'erlooked** bewitched

18 **naughty** worthless (*related to 'nought'*)

19 **bars** obstacles

20 **though yours, not yours** Portia 'belongs to' Bassanio (*because she has given him her heart); but does not properly belong to him until he wins her by choosing the right casket.*

20–21 **Prove it so...not I** *If Bassanio chooses the wrong casket, at least Portia will not have broken her oath: bad luck will be to blame.*

22 **peize** slow down

23 **eche** stretch out (*to make it last longer*)

24 **to stay...election** to delay you making your choice

25 **the rack** *an instrument of torture; the word leads Portia to the idea of people being made to confess treason (lines 26–27) and saying anything to save themselves (lines 32–33)*

29 **fear th' enjoying** worry that I might never enjoy

30 **amity** fear

33 **enforcèd** being forced (*by torture*)

Portia (Helen Schlesinger), Bassanio (Scott Handy) and the caskets (RSC 1997)

Scene 2

Belmont. A room in Portia's house.

Enter BASSANIO, PORTIA, GRATIANO, NERISSA, *and all their trains.*

PORTIA	I pray you, tarry; pause a day or two	
	Before you hazard, for in choosing wrong	
	I lose your company; therefore forbear a while.	
	There's something tells me – but it is not love –	
	I would not lose you; and you know yourself,	5
	Hate counsels not in such a quality.	
	But lest you should not understand me well –	
	And yet a maiden hath no tongue but thought –	
	I would detain you here some month or two	
	Before you venture for me. I could teach you	10
	How to choose right, but then I am forsworn;	
	So will I never be; so may you miss me;	
	But if you do, you'll make me wish a sin,	
	That I had been forsworn. Beshrew your eyes;	
	They have o'erlooked me and divided me;	15
	One half of me is yours, the other half yours –	
	Mine own I would say; but if mine, then yours,	
	And so all yours. O, these naughty times	
	Put bars between the owners and their rights!	
	And so though yours, not yours. Prove it so,	20
	Let fortune go to hell for it, not I.	
	I speak too long, but 't is to peize the time,	
	To eche it, and to draw it out in length,	
	To stay you from election.	

BASSANIO   Let me choose,
For as I am, I live upon the rack.   25

PORTIA   Upon the rack, Bassanio? then confess
What treason there is mingled with your love.

BASSANIO   None but that ugly treason of mistrust,
Which makes me fear th' enjoying of my love.
There may as well be amity and life   30
'Tween snow and fire, as treason and my love.

PORTIA   Ay, but I fear you speak upon the rack
Where men enforcèd do speak anything.

3.2 Belmont: Portia's house

After thinking seriously about the inscriptions, Bassanio realises that appearances can often be deceptive and chooses the lead casket, rejecting the superficial attractiveness of gold and silver.

70 **knell** death bell

73 **So may...themselves** so appearances can be deceptive

74 **with ornament** by outside appearances

76 **seasoned** made to sound acceptable

78 **sober brow** serious-faced person

79 **approve...text** support it by quoting from the Bible

81–82 **assumes...parts** takes on some outward appearance of good

83–86 **How many...milk?** think about all the lily-livered cowards there are who look as brave as legendary heroes

87 **valour's excrement** 'a brave man's beard'; the appearance of bravery (**excrement** = outgrowth)

88 **render them redoubted** make them look fearsome

89 **purchased by the weight** *Cosmetics and false hair were bought by the ounce.*

91 **lightest** *word-play:* (1) weighing least; (2) most immodest

92 **crispèd** curled

snaky (1) sinuous; (2) deceitful

93 **wanton gambols** carefree (and irresponsible) dances

94 **Upon...fairness** placed on top of false beauty

95 **dowry...head** *a wig made from the hair of someone who has died*

96 **sepulchre** tomb

97 **guilèd** treacherous

99 **Indian** dark-skinned (*in Shakespeare's time dark skin was not fashionable; women copied Queen Elizabeth, who was fair-skinned*)

102 **Midas** *the legendary king who made a wish that everything he touched would turn to gold; he had not realised that this would apply to food and drink*

103 **common drudge** servant at everyone's command (*coins were made of silver*)

104 **meagre** poor, barren

105 **aught** anything

106 **eloquence** fine talking

<table>
<tr><td></td><td>Let us all ring Fancy's knell;</td><td>70</td></tr>
<tr><td></td><td>I'll begin it – Ding, dong, bell.</td><td></td></tr>
<tr><td>ALL</td><td>Ding, dong, bell.</td><td></td></tr>
</table>

BASSANIO	So may the outward shows be least themselves;	
	The world is still deceived with ornament.	
	In law, what plea so tainted and corrupt,	75
	But, being seasoned with a gracious voice,	
	Obscures the show of evil? In religion,	
	What damnèd error but some sober brow	
	Will bless it, and approve it with a text,	
	Hiding the grossness with fair ornament?	80
	There is no vice so simple, but assumes	
	Some mark of virtue on his outward parts.	
	How many cowards whose hearts are all as false	
	As stairs of sand, wear yet upon their chins	
	The beards of Hercules and frowning Mars,	85
	Who, inward searched, have livers white as milk?	
	And these assume but valour's excrement	
	To render them redoubted. Look on beauty,	
	And you shall see 't is purchased by the weight,	
	Which therein works a miracle in nature,	90
	Making them lightest that wear most of it;	
	So are those crispèd, snaky golden locks	
	Which make such wanton gambols with the wind	
	Upon supposèd fairness, often known	
	To be the dowry of a second head,	95
	The skull that bred them in the sepulchre.	
	Thus ornament is but the guilèd shore	
	To a most dangerous sea, the beauteous scarf	
	Veiling an Indian beauty – in a word,	
	The seeming truth which cunning times put	
	on	100
	To entrap the wisest. Therefore, thou gaudy gold,	
	Hard food for Midas, I will none of thee,	
	Nor none of thee, thou pale and common drudge	
	'Tween man and man. But thou, thou meagre lead,	
	Which rather threaten'st than dost promise aught,	105
	Thy paleness moves me more than eloquence,	
	And here choose I; joy be the consequence!	

3.2 Belmont: Portia's house

Portia tells Bassanio that she and all her wealth and possessions are now his. She gives him a ring, saying that, if he ever loses it or gives it away, it will mean that he has stopped loving her.

Activities

Character review: Portia (4)

Her view of herself
When Bassanio chooses the correct casket, Portia gives a very modest statement about herself (lines 149–171).

A List the main points of her speech. What exactly does she say about:
- wanting to be better than she is, for his sake (lines 150–157)
- her own weaknesses and deficiencies (lines 157–159)
- her willingness to be ruled by Bassanio (lines 159–165)
- her readiness to hand over all her property to him (lines 166–171)?

B What are Bassanio's reactions to Portia's speech? Write down his thoughts and feelings, paying attention to each of the four points highlighted in **A** above.

C What is your opinion of Portia's behaviour here? Draft a written response to someone who said, 'I completely lose all respect for Portia in this speech. How can she possibly grovel in this way, calling herself "an unlessoned girl, unschooled, unpractised", and offering to be "directed As from her lord, her governor, her king"? It's humiliating.' (You are allowed to agree or disagree!)

146 **thrice-fair** beautiful three times over

148 **ratified** officially approved

150–152 **though for…better** though I do not want to be better than I am, merely to satisfy my own ambitions

155 **That** so that

account estimation

156 **livings** possessions

157 **Exceed account** be too high a figure to calculate

158 **to term in gross** (1) to name it in total; (2) to describe it bluntly

166–167 **Myself and…converted** *Portia is handing over herself and all her possessions to Bassanio.*

167 **But now** only a moment ago

169 **even now** in this very moment

173 **presage** foretell

174 **vantage to…you** opportunity to accuse you

175 **bereft** robbed

176 **blood** passions

177 **powers** ability to speak or think

178 **oration** public speech

181–183 **Where every…expressed** where everything mixed up together comes out as a confused sound, conveying only a general idea of happiness

Giddy in spirit, still gazing in a doubt
Whether those peals of praise be his or no,   145
So, thrice-fair lady, stand I even so,
As doubtful whether what I see be true,
Until confirmed, signed, ratified by you.

PORTIA   You see me, Lord Bassanio, where I stand,
Such as I am; though for myself alone   150
I would not be ambitious in my wish
To wish myself much better, yet for you,
I would be trebled twenty times myself,
A thousand times more fair, ten thousand times
          more rich,
That only to stand high in your account,   155
I might in virtues, beauties, livings, friends
Exceed account. But the full sum of me
Is sum of – something: which, to term in gross,
Is an unlessoned girl, unschooled, unpractised;
Happy in this, she is not yet so old   160
But she may learn; happier than this,
She is not bred so dull but she can learn;
Happiest of all, is that her gentle spirit
Commits itself to yours to be directed,
As from her lord, her governor, her king.   165
Myself, and what is mine, to you and yours
Is now converted. But now I was the lord
Of this fair mansion, master of my servants,
Queen o'er myself; and even now, but now,
This house, these servants, and this same myself   170
Are yours, my lord! I give them with this ring,
Which when you part from, lose, or give away,
Let it presage the ruin of your love,
And be my vantage to exclaim on you.

BASSANIO   Madam, you have bereft me of all words;   175
Only my blood speaks to you in my veins,
And there is such confusion in my powers,
As after some oration fairly spoke
By a belovèd prince, there doth appear
Among the buzzing pleasèd multitude –   180
Where every something being blent together,
Turns to a wild of nothing, save of joy
Expressed, and not expressed. But when this ring

3.2 Belmont: Portia's house

As the two couples are sharing a joke, Lorenzo, Jessica and Salerio arrive from Venice. Gratiano tells Salerio about their successful wooing and asks for news of Antonio.

Activities

Actors' interpretations: a change of mood

After the joyous celebrations, there is a change of mood. Create two a freeze-frames. The first represents the scene at line 218: the four lovers are celebrating and reacting in their separate ways to Gratiano's joke, as Lorenzo, Jessica and Salerio arrive unexpectedly. How do the visitors look? Are they pleased to see such happiness, or do their concerns for Antonio show in their expressions?

The second freeze-frame is for line 241. Gratiano has happily greeted Salerio with the news of their success, but receives a worrying reply. Check what the other characters are doing: Bassanio, Portia and Nerissa particularly (and look at the activity below).

Actors' interpretations: Antonio's letter

It will help Bassanio in the freeze-frame if he has a letter to read. What do you think Antonio would say in his letter to Bassanio? (Draft a version and, once you have written it – maximum sixty words – compare it with the actual letter at the end of the scene.)

217 **infidel** non-Christian

220–221 **If that...welcome** if I have the authority to extend a welcome – given that I have only just become the master here

228 **did entreat...nay** begged me so forcefully that it was impossible to refuse

231 **Commends him** sends his greetings

Ere I ope before I open

233–234 **Not sick...mind** he is not physically ill; any changes have been to his psychological health

235 **his estate** the condition he is in

236 **yon stranger** the new-comer over there (*Jessica*)

240 **Jasons** *see note to 1.1.170*

241 **would** wish

GRATIANO   No, we shall ne'er win at that sport and stake down.
           But who comes here? Lorenzo and his infidel!
           What! and my old Venetian friend Salerio?

Enter LORENZO, JESSICA, *and* SALERIO.

BASSANIO   Lorenzo and Salerio, welcome hither,
           If that the youth of my new int'rest here   220
           Have power to bid you welcome. By your leave
           I bid my very friends and countrymen,
           Sweet Portia, welcome.

PORTIA   So do I my lord;
           They are entirely welcome.

LORENZO   I thank your honour. For my part, my lord,   225
           My purpose was not to have seen you here,
           But meeting with Salerio by the way,
           He did entreat me, past all saying nay,
           To come with him along.

SALERIO   I did, my lord,
           And I have reason for it. Signior Antonio   230
           Commends him to you.

He gives BASSANIO *a letter.*

BASSANIO   Ere I ope his letter,
           I pray you tell me how my good friend doth.

SALERIO   Not sick, my lord, unless it be in mind,
           Nor well, unless in mind; his letter there
           Will show you his estate.   235

BASSANIO *opens the letter.*

GRATIANO   Nerissa, cheer yon stranger, bid her welcome.
           Your hand, Salerio (*They shake hands*) what's the
               news from Venice?
           How doth that royal merchant, good Antonio?
           I know he will be glad of our success;
           We are the Jasons, we have won the fleece.   240

SALERIO   I would you had won the fleece that he hath lost.

3.2 Belmont: Portia's house

Bassanio is shocked when he reads Antonio's letter, and he tells Portia about his debts to Antonio, the bond with Shylock and the loss of Antonio's ships. Salerio confirms the account of Antonio's losses and reports that Shylock is demanding justice.

242 **shrewd** evil

245–246 **turn...man** alter the appearance of a stable and healthy man

247 **With leave** with your permission

252 **impart my love to you** tell you I loved you

253–254 **all the wealth...veins** the only wealth I had was in my blood (*he came from a 'good' family, but has no material possessions*)

256 **Rating** estimating

257 **braggart** boaster

260 **have engaged myself** am in debt to

261 **mere** absolute

262 **feed my means** provide me with what I need

266 **ventures** business deals, investments

hit success

267 **Tripolis...** *see note to 1.3.16*

268 **Barbary** *north-west Africa*

269 **scape** escaped

270 **merchant-marring rocks** rocks which ruin merchants (*by destroying their ships*)

272 **discharge** pay off

275 **confound** destroy

276 **plies the duke** pesters the duke with requests

277 **doth impeach...justice** he claims there is no justice in Venice, if he is not allowed to pursue his case

279–280 **magnificoes...port** most important magnates; powerful businessmen

Bassanio (Scott Handy) reading Antonio's letter (RSC 1997)

PORTIA	There are some shrewd contents in yon same paper,
	That steals the colour from Bassanio's cheek –
	Some dear friend dead, else nothing in the world
	Could turn so much the constitution 245
	Of any constant man. What, worse and worse?
	With leave, Bassanio, I am half yourself,
	And I must freely have the half of anything
	That this same paper brings you.
BASSANIO	O sweet Portia,
	Here are a few of the unpleasant'st words 250
	That ever blotted paper! Gentle lady,
	When I did first impart my love to you,
	I freely told you all the wealth I had
	Ran in my veins – I was a gentleman;
	And then I told you true. And yet, dear lady, 255
	Rating myself at nothing, you shall see
	How much I was a braggart. When I told you
	My state was nothing, I should then have told you
	That I was worse than nothing; for indeed
	I have engaged myself to a dear friend, 260
	Engaged my friend to his mere enemy
	To feed my means. Here is a letter, lady;
	The paper as the body of my friend,
	And every word in it a gaping wound
	Issuing life-blood. But is it true, Salerio? 265
	Hath all his ventures failed? what, not one hit?
	From Tripolis, from Mexico, and England,
	From Lisbon, Barbary, and India,
	And not one vessel scape the dreadful touch
	Of merchant-marring rocks?
SALERIO	Not one, my lord. 270
	Besides, it should appear that if he had
	The present money to discharge the Jew,
	He would not take it. Never did I know
	A creature that did bear the shape of man
	So keen and greedy to confound a man. 275
	He plies the duke at morning and at night,
	And doth impeach the freedom of the state
	If they deny him justice. Twenty merchants,
	The duke himself, and the magnificoes
	Of greatest port have all persuaded with him, 280

3.3 Near Shylock's house

Bassanio reads Antonio's letter to Portia and promises to return as soon as he can. In Venice, Antonio has persuaded the gaoler to let him come out of prison to approach Shylock; but Shylock will not listen to pleas for mercy.

Activities

Shakespeare's language: ambiguity

One of the things that actors love about Shakespeare's language is its ambiguity – the fact that it can have many different meanings. This allows actors to interpret things in different ways. Two of Portia's lines here are interestingly ambiguous.

In line 312 she says to Bassanio, 'Since you are dear bought, I will love you dear.' This could mean (among other things): (a) Since you have cost me a lot of money…; or (b) Since Antonio's loan has proved costly to him…

Shortly afterwards, hearing the words in Antonio's letter, she exclaims 'O love, dispatch all business and be gone!' (line 321). Usually actresses say 'O love', rather like 'O darling'. But in the 1997 Globe production, Kathryn Pogson smiled knowingly and said, as though commenting on the relationship between Antonio and Bassanio, 'Oh…! Love!' ('Oh, I see it all now…He loves him!')

Say both these ambiguous lines aloud and decide in each case which meaning you prefer (or find further meanings of your own).

315–316 **my bond…is forfeit** *Antonio has failed to repay the loan and Shylock can now enforce the pound-of-flesh clause.*

318–319 **Notwithstanding…pleasure** despite that, follow your own inclinations (do as you wish)

321 **dispatch all business** finish making arrangements here

322 **good leave** permission

324 **stay** delay

325 **Nor rest…twain** rest will not come between the two of us (I will not rest until I see you again)

2 **gratis** without charging interest (*Latin for 'free'*)

9 **naughty** worthless (*see note to 3.2.18*)

art so fond are so foolish

10 **come abroad** walk the streets; come out of gaol

14 **dull-eyed** not perceptive; gullible

the Jew is forfeit, and, since in paying it, it is impossible
I should live, all debts are cleared between you and I, if
I might but see you at my death. Notwithstanding, use
your pleasure; if your love do not persuade you to come,
let not my letter.   320

PORTIA   O love, dispatch all business and be gone!

BASSANIO   Since I have your good leave to go away,
I will make haste; but, till I come again,
No bed shall e'er be guilty of my stay,
Nor rest be interposer 'twixt us twain.   325

                                                 Exeunt.

Scene 3

Venice. A street.

Enter SHYLOCK *the Jew, with* SOLANIO, *and* ANTONIO, *and a*
GAOLER.

SHYLOCK   Gaoler, look to him; tell not me of mercy;
This is the fool that lent out money gratis.
Gaoler, look to him

ANTONIO   Hear me yet, good Shylock.

SHYLOCK   I'll have my bond; speak not against my bond!
I have sworn an oath that I will have my bond.   5
Thou call'dst me dog before thou hadst a cause,
But since I am a dog, beware my fangs.
The duke shall grant me justice. I do wonder,
Thou naughty gaoler, that thou art so fond
To come abroad with him at his request.   10

ANTONIO   I pray thee hear me speak.

SHYLOCK   I'll have my bond. I will not hear thee speak;
I'll have my bond, and therefore speak no more.
I'll not be made a soft and dull-eyed fool,
To shake the head, relent, and sigh, and yield   15

3.4 Belmont: Portia's house

Portia temporarily hands over control of her house to Lorenzo and Jessica, explaining that she and Nerissa are planning to stay in a nearby monastery until their husbands return.

Activities

Character review: Jessica (3)

Her one line
Jessica speaks only one line here ('I wish your ladyship all heart's content', line 42) and many directors have taken this to mean that she is shy and nervous.

In threes, act out lines 40–44, with Jessica saying her line as though she were:

- completely overawed at the thought of being put in charge of Portia's household
- worshipping Portia
- not knowing how to react and simply copying Lorenzo's behaviour
- and other ways you can think of.

Then write a continuation of her letter to Venice (see page 106) in which she expresses how she feels being put in charge of this impressive household.

9 **Than customary…you** than day-to-day kindness requires you to perform

10 **repent for** regret

13 **bear an egall yoke of love** love each other equally, mutually

14 **There needs…proportion** there has to be a similar balance

15 **lineaments** physical features

17 **bosom lover** close friend (*in Shakespeare's* Julius Cæsar, *Brutus refers to Cæsar as his 'best lover'*)

19–21 **How little…cruelty** if Antonio is so like Bassanio, I regard it as a small expense to have rescued him from his cruel torment

25 **husbandry and manage** care and management

28 **contemplation** meditation

32 **abide** stay

33 **imposition** task imposed upon you

34 **The which** which

37 **my people** my servants (*Portia's household*)

38 **acknowledge you…** regard you as the master and mistress

How true a gentleman you send relief,
How dear a lover of my lord your husband,
I know you would be prouder of the work
Than customary bounty can enforce you.

PORTIA I never did repent for doing good,   10
Nor shall not now; for in companions
That do converse and waste the time together,
Whose souls do bear an egall yoke of love,
There must be needs a like proportion
Of lineaments, of manners, and of spirit;   15
Which makes me think that this Antonio,
Being the bosom lover of my lord,
Must needs be like my lord. If it be so,
How little is the cost I have bestowed
In purchasing the semblance of my soul   20
From out the state of hellish cruelty!
This comes too near the praising of myself;
Therefore no more of it; hear other things.
Lorenzo, I commit into your hands
The husbandry and manage of my house,   25
Until my lord's return. For mine own part,
I have toward heaven breathed a secret vow
To live in prayer and contemplation,
Only attended by Nerissa here,
Until her husband and my lord's return.   30
There is a monastery two miles off,
And there we will abide. I do desire you
Not to deny this imposition,
The which my love and some necessity
Now lays upon you.

LORENZO   Madam, with all my heart,   35
I shall obey you in all fair commands.

PORTIA My people do already know my mind,
And will acknowledge you and Jessica
In place of Lord Bassanio and myself.
So fare you well till we shall meet again.   40

LORENZO Fair thoughts and happy hours attend on you!

JESSICA I wish your ladyship all heart's content.

3.4 Belmont: Portia's house

Portia sends her servant Balthazar to Padua with a letter for her lawyer cousin, Doctor Bellario, asking for some law books and courtroom dress. She plans to disguise herself and Nerissa as young male lawyers and journey to Venice in an attempt to help Antonio.

Activities

Shakespeare's language: mockery and satire

Portia seems to enjoy mocking the way young men swagger about, bragging of their fights and the women who have fallen in love with them (lines 62–78). What would Portia say about young men's behaviour if she were alive today? Draft a modern version of her speech, making it as witty and as satirical as you can.

Debra Gillett as Nerissa (holding letter) and Penny Downie as Portia in the RSC 1993 production

46 **honest-true** faithful
49 **Padua** *a city famous for its university and law school*
   render give
51 **look what** whatever
52 **with imagined speed** as fast as possible
53 **traject** ferry
54 **trades to** communicates with
56 **convenient** appropriate
60 **a habit** clothes
61–62 **we are accomplished…lack** we are equipped with what we lack (*i.e. male genitals*)
62 **wager** bet
63 **accoutered** kitted out
65 **the braver grace** more style
66 **between the change…boy** as though my voice were changing
67 **reed** piping, high-pitched
   mincing dainty
68 **frays** fights
69 **quaint** (1) clever; (2) to do with sex
71 **Which I denying** and when I rejected them
72 **could not do withal** couldn't help it
74 **puny** pathetic
75–76 **discontinued…twelvemonth** left school over a year ago
77 **raw** immature
   Jacks lads

PORTIA   I thank you for your wish, and am well pleased
         To wish it back on you; fare you well, Jessica.

                                    Exeunt JESSICA *and* LORENZO.

         Now Balthazar,   45
         As I have ever found thee honest-true,
         So let me find thee still. Take this same letter,
         And use thou all th' endeavour of a man
         In speed to Padua. See thou render this
         Into my cousin's hand, Doctor Bellario,   50
         And look what notes and garments he doth give thee.
         Bring them, I pray thee, with imagined speed
         Unto the traject, to the common ferry
         Which trades to Venice; waste no time in words,
         But get thee gone! I shall be there before thee. 55

BALTHAZAR   Madam, I go with all convenient speed.

                                                           Exit.

PORTIA   Come on, Nerissa, I have work in hand
         That you yet know not of; we'll see our husbands
         Before they think of us!

NERISSA   Shall they see us?

PORTIA   They shall, Nerissa, but in such a habit   60
         That they shall think we are accomplished
         With that we lack. I'll hold thee any wager,
         When we are both accoutered like young men,
         I'll prove the prettier fellow of the two,
         And wear my dagger with the braver grace,   65
         And speak between the change of man and boy,
         With a reed voice, and turn two mincing steps
         Into a manly stride, and speak of frays
         Like a fine bragging youth; and tell quaint lies
         How honourable ladies sought my love,   70
         Which I denying, they fell sick and died.
         I could not do withal. Then I'll repent.
         And wish, for all that, that I had not killed them.
         And twenty of these puny lies I'll tell,
         That men shall swear I have discontinued school   75
         Above a twelvemonth. I have within my mind
         A thousand raw tricks of these bragging Jacks

3.5 Belmont: Portia's house

Lorenzo enters just as Launcelot is complaining that all these Jews converting to Christianity are putting up the price of pork and bacon! Lorenzo accuses Launcelot of having got one of the servants pregnant.

Activities

Themes: anti-Semitism (2)

Although Launcelot's conversation with Jessica is usually played in a light-hearted way, there were people in Shakespeare's time who would take his comments seriously, as there was a widespread irrational hatred of Jews (see pages 200–201 and the activity on page 70). Find the points where Launcelot seems to be echoing the following beliefs commonly held by Christians at that time:

- People are punished for sins committed by their parents and grandparents.
- Anyone who is not a Christian is damned and will go to hell.
- Jews who convert to Christianity are saved from damnation.
- Too many Jews are converting to Christianity: there are enough Christians already.

In pairs, perform the exchange (lines 1–25), first as though Launcelot is perfectly serious; then jokingly. Which version seems to work best? (Think about the relationship between Launcelot and Jessica, as we have seen it in 2.3, for example.)

22 **enow** enough

22–23 **e'en as many…another** just as many as could live happily side-by-side

23–24 **raise the price of hogs** *because Christians eat pigs (***hogs***) and Jews do not*

24–25 **rasher…for money** soon we won't be able to afford a rasher of bacon to cook over the fire

31 **are out** have quarrelled

34 **the commonwealth** the state; society

37 **getting up…belly** *Launcelot seems to have got 'the Moor' pregnant; but we do not hear about it after this scene (***Moor:** *see note to the opening stage directions of 2.1).*

39 **much** appropriate

more than reason bigger than she should be

42–45 **the best grace…parrots** soon the most highly regarded form of wit will be silence, leaving all the talking to parrots (*people like Launcelot who repeat other people's words without understanding them*)

47 **have stomachs** are hungry

50 **"cover"** lay the table

52 **Not so…duty** *'cover' also means 'wear a hat'; Launcelot points out that it would be wrong to do so in their presence*

enow before, e'en as many as could well live one
by another. This making of Christians will raise the
price of hogs – if we grow all to be pork-eaters, we
shall not shortly have a rasher on the coals for
money.   25

Enter LORENZO.

JESSICA   I'll tell my husband, Launcelot, what you say; here
              he comes!

LORENZO   I shall grow jealous of you shortly, Launcelot, if
              you thus get my wife into corners!

JESSICA   Nay, you need not fear us, Lorenzo; Launcelot and   30
              I are out. He tells me flatly there's no mercy for me
              in heaven, because I am a Jew's daughter; and he
              says you are no good member of the
              commonwealth, for in converting Jews to
              Christians you raise the price of pork.   35

LORENZO   I shall answer that better to the commonwealth
              than you can the getting up of the negro's belly; the
              Moor is with child by you, Launcelot!

LAUNCELOT   It is much that the Moor should be more than
              reason; but if she be less than an honest woman,   40
              she is indeed more than I took her for.

LORENZO   How every fool can play upon the word! I think the
              best grace of wit will shortly turn into silence, and
              discourse grow commendable in none only but
              parrots. Go in, sirrah; bid them prepare for   45
              dinner!

LAUNCELOT   That is done, sir; they have all stomachs!

LORENZO   Goodly Lord, what a wit-snapper are you! then bid
              them prepare dinner!

LAUNCELOT   That is done too, sir, only "cover" is the word.   50

LORENZO   Will you cover then, sir?

LAUNCELOT   Not so, sir, neither; I know my duty.

3.5 Belmont: Portia's house

Jessica and Lorenzo go in to dinner, joking with each other.

Activities

Character review: Lorenzo and Jessica (1)

What is your impression of the relationship between Lorenzo and Jessica? In some productions, they are not portrayed as a totally happy couple. Talk together about each of the following statements, deciding whether you agree with them or not:

(a) Lorenzo is jealous of Jessica's close relationship with Launcelot (lines 28–29)

(b) Lorenzo rebukes Launcelot for getting 'the moor' pregnant, in order to show him up in front of Jessica (lines 36–38)

(c) Launcelot's word-play when he is told to prepare the dinner is his way of getting back at Lorenzo and showing his superiority (lines 47–62)

(d) when Lorenzo boasts that he is as excellent a husband as Portia is a wife, he is perfectly serious (lines 81–82).

Pick a section of the scene and act it out, first as though Lorenzo and Jessica are perfectly happy together, then as though there is a great deal of tension in their relationship. Talk about which version seems to fit your overall interpretation of the play.

87 **howsome'er thou speak'st** however you speak about me

88 **digest** *Lorenzo picks up Jessica's word-play of 'stomach' (line 82):* **digest** *also means 'understand'*

set you forth *more word-play on 'set forth':* (1) praise greatly; (2) 'dish up' (*a meal*)

LORENZO   No, pray thee, let it serve for table-talk;
               Then, howsome'er thou speak'st, 'mong other things
               I shall digest it.

JESSICA   Well, I'll set you forth.

Exeunt.

4.1 Venice: the Duke's palace

In the Duke's palace, Antonio presents himself before the court and the Duke expresses his sympathy. When Shylock enters, the Duke tries to persuade him to show mercy and drop the case against Antonio.

Activities

Themes: justice and mercy (1)

Look back at 3.3. In that scene, Shylock insists on his legal right to pursue the case against Antonio – 'I will have my bond' – and refuses to listen to any pleas that he should show mercy.

When Act 4 opens, we learn that the Duke has been trying to persuade Shylock to 'qualify His rigorous course', but that Shylock 'stands obdurate' (lines 8–9).

Write a letter from the Duke to Shylock in which he tries to persuade him to show mercy to Antonio. Then write a brief reply from Shylock in which he talks about justice and his bond.

2 **Ready** (1) 'Present!'; (2) prepared

3 **answer** defend yourself against

4 **stony adversary** hard-hearted enemy

5 **Uncapable of** unable to feel
   void empty

6 **dram** tiny amount

7–8 **qualify...course** moderate the harshness of his intentions

8 **stands obdurate** remains unmoved

10 **envy** malice; evil intentions

13 **tyranny** cruelty

18 **thou...this fashion** you are only keeping up the pretence

19 **hour of act** moment

20 **remorse** pity, compassion

20–21 **strange** *line 20:* wonderful; *line 21:* extraordinary

22 **exact'st** demand

24 **loose the forfeiture** release him from paying the penalty (*his flesh*)

24 **a portion of the principal** *part of the original three thousand ducats that he borrowed*

28 **of late** recently

Act 4

4.1

Scene 1

Venice. A Court of Justice.

Enter the DUKE, *the Magnificoes* ANTONIO, BASSANIO, *and* GRATIANO, SALERIO *and others.*

DUKE What, is Antonio here?

ANTONIO Ready, so please your grace!

DUKE I am sorry for thee; thou art come to answer
A stony adversary, an inhuman wretch,
Uncapable of pity, void and empty   5
From any dram of mercy.

ANTONIO   I have heard
Your grace hath ta'en great pains to qualify
His rigorous course; but since he stands obdurate,
And that no lawful means can carry me
Out of his envy's reach, I do oppose   10
My patience to his fury, and am armed
To suffer with a quietness of spirit
The very tyranny and rage of his.

DUKE Go, one, call the Jew into the court.

SALERIO He is ready at the door; he comes, my lord.   15

Enter SHYLOCK.

DUKE Make room, and let him stand before our face.
Shylock, the world thinks, and I think so too,
That thou but leadest this fashion of thy malice
To the last hour of act, and then 't is thought
Thou'lt show thy mercy and remorse, more
     strange   20
Than is thy strange apparent cruelty;
And where thou now exact'st the penalty,
Which is a pound of this poor merchant's flesh,
Thou wilt not only loose the forfeiture,
But, touched with human gentleness and love,   25
Forgive a moiety of the principal,
Glancing an eye of pity on his losses
That have of late so huddled on his back

127

4.1 Venice: the Duke's palace

Shylock rejects the Duke's pleas for mercy and explains why he is pursuing the case: he has sworn an oath to exact the penalty, he says, and he refuses to give any reason for his actions, other than his hatred for Antonio.

29 **Enow** enough

30–33 **And pluck...courtesy** and draw some pity for his situation from hard-hearted people who have not been brought up to view kindness as a duty

32 **Tartars** *war-like people from central Asia; like Turks, they were non-Christians, and therefore, in the Duke's opinion, did not value qualities such as mercy and forgiveness*

34 **gentle** *with a probable pun on 'gentile'; see 1.3.173 and 2.4.35*

35 **possessed** informed

36 **Sabbath** *the Jewish holy day*

37 **due and forfeit** the money which is due to me

38 **danger light** harm fall

39 **charter** privileges as a city

41 **carrion** rotting

43 **it is my humou**r *either:* (1) it's the mood I'm in ('because I feel like it'); *or:* (2) it's in my character ('a fixation of mine')

46 **baned** poisoned

47 **gaping pig** roasted pig with its mouth open (*as a Jew, Shylock does not eat pork*)

49 **sings i' the nose** makes a whining nasal sound

50–52 **affection...loathes** our natural response, which controls our emotions, causes us to react with either love or hate

53 **no firm...rendered** no right answer which can be given

56 **of force** involuntarily

57–58 **must yield...offend** has to give in to the embarrassment of wetting himself

60 **lodged** fixed, immovable

certain steadfast

62 **A losing suit** an unprofitable case (*because, even if he wins, he will not get his money back*)

64 **current** course, direction

67 **Hates...kill?** do you let things live if you hate them?

Enow to press a royal merchant down,
And pluck commiseration of his state   30
From brassy bosoms and rough hearts of flint,
From stubborn Turks, and Tartars never trained
To offices of tender courtesy.
We all expect a gentle answer, Jew!

SHYLOCK   I have possessed your grace of what I purpose,   35
And by our holy Sabbath have I sworn
To have the due and forfeit of my bond.
If you deny it, let the danger light
Upon your charter and your city's freedom!
You'll ask me why I rather choose to have   40
A weight of carrion flesh than to receive
Three thousand ducats. I'll not answer that!
But say it is my humour – is it answered?
What if my house be troubled with a rat,
And I be pleased to give ten thousand ducats   45
To have it baned? What, are you answered yet?
Some men there are love not a gaping pig;
Some that are mad if they behold a cat;
And others, when the bagpipe sings i' th' nose,
Cannot contain their urine – for affection,   50
Master of passion, sways it to the mood
Of what it likes or loathes, Now for your answer:
As there is no firm reason to be rendered
Why *he* cannot abide a gaping pig,
Why *he* a harmless, necessary cat,   55
Why *he* a woollen bagpipe, but of force
Must yield to such inevitable shame
As to offend, himself being offended;
So can I give no reason, nor I will not,
More than a lodged hate and a certain loathing   60
I bear Antonio, that I follow thus
A losing suit against him! Are you answered?

BASSANIO   This is no answer, thou unfeeling man,
To excuse the current of thy cruelty.

SHYLOCK   I am not bound to please thee with my answers!   65

BASSANIO   Do all men kill the things they do not love?

SHYLOCK   Hates any man the thing he would not kill?

4.1 Venice: the Duke's palace

Antonio realises that it is pointless trying to persuade Shylock to show mercy and asks for the case to proceed. Shylock rejects Bassanio's offer of twice the sum owed and argues that his demand for a pound of Antonio's flesh is a fair one, in line with the laws of Venice.

Activities

Character review: Shylock (12)

'say it is my humour'
What points does Shylock put forward to explain why he is claiming a pound of Antonio's flesh, rather than three thousand ducats? Re-read lines 40–62:

- What does he mean by 'say it is my humour' (line 43)?
- What does he compare the destruction of Antonio with (lines 44–46)?
- Which three examples does he give to explain his point about irrational hatreds and phobias?
- How does he conclude his argument (lines 59–62)?

Themes: anti-Semitism (4)

'His Jewish heart'
In Antonio's bitter reply to the court (lines 70–83), he uses the word 'Jew' or 'Jewish' three times (lines 70, 80 and 83).

Look carefully at each use of the word and decide whether Antonio is being anti-Semitic. In other words, is he using 'Jew' and 'Jewish' as insults? Is he suggesting that Shylock is mean and vengeful mainly because he is a Jew?

68 **Every offence...** you don't hate someone just for offending you once

70 **think you question** bear in mind that you are arguing with

72 **bid the main flood bate** ask the high tide to decrease

73 **use question with** inquire of

76 **wag** sway

77 **fretten** fretted; annoyed

81 **farther means** further methods

82 **with all brief...conveniency** being as brief and as clear as you can be

87 **draw** take

88 **rendering** giving

92 **in abject...parts** to do menial jobs only fit for slaves

95 **burthens** burdens

96–97 **let their palates...viands** let them enjoy the same kinds of food as you

101 **fie upon your law!** your law is worthless!

102 **decrees** laws

104 **Upon my power...court** it is within my powers to dismiss the court (*and give the judgement in favour of Shylock*)

BASSANIO	Every offence is not a hate at first!
SHYLOCK	What! wouldst thou have a serpent sting thee twice?
ANTONIO	I pray you think you question with the Jew. 70
	You may as well go stand upon the beach
	And bid the main flood bate his usual height;
	You may as well use question with the wolf,
	Why he hath made the ewe bleat for the lamb;
	You may as well forbid the mountain pines 75
	To wag their high tops, and to make no noise
	When they are fretten with the gusts of heaven;
	You may as well do anything most hard
	As seek to soften that – than which what's harder?
	His Jewish heart! Therefore, I do beseech you, 80
	Make no more offers, use no farther means,
	But with all brief and plain conveniency
	Let me have judgement, and the Jew his will!
BASSANIO	For thy three thousand ducats, here is six!
SHYLOCK	If every ducat in six thousand ducats 85
	Were in six parts, and every part a ducat,
	I would not draw them; I would have my bond!
DUKE	How shalt thou hope for mercy, rendering none?
SHYLOCK	What judgement shall I dread, doing no wrong?
	You have among you many a purchased slave, 90
	Which, like your asses, and your dogs and mules,
	You use in abject and in slavish parts.
	Because you bought them; shall I say to you,
	Let them be free, marry them to your heirs?
	Why sweat they under burthens? let their beds 95
	Be made as soft as yours, and let their palates
	Be seasoned with such viands? You will answer
	"The slaves are ours." So do I answer you:
	The pound of flesh which I demand of him
	Is dearly bought, 't is mine and I will have it; 100
	If you deny me, fie upon your law!
	There is no force in the decrees of Venice!
	I stand for judgement; answer, shall I have it?
DUKE	Upon my power I may dismiss this court,

4.1 Venice: the Duke's palace

Shylock remains unmoved by Gratiano's insults. The Duke reads out Bellario's letter: he is ill, but in his place he has sent a young lawyer called Balthazar, who understands all about the case. Portia enters, disguised as the lawyer, Balthazar.

Activities

Actors' interpretations: animals

Gratiano claims that Shylock has inherited the soul of a wolf, and elsewhere in the play he is called 'dog' or 'cur'. Many actors find that it helps to think of their character as a particular animal. Philip Voss, who played Shylock in 1997, said, 'Of course, wolf is the obvious animal, and maybe it should be a wolf. But there's something cackling and scavenging about Shylock, and the animal I'm sticking with is a hyena.' Which would you prefer for Shylock – wolf, dog, hyena, or something different?

Launcelot Gobbo is accused of being a parrot at one point (3.5.41–44). Which animals fit your own interpretation of the other major characters, such as Antonio and Portia?

David Calder as Shylock (RSC 1993)

135 **fell** cruel

fleet flit; fly off

136 **unhallowed dam** cursed mother

137 **Infused** seeped into

139 **Till thou...loud** until your ranting can remove the seal from my bond, you are only hurting your lungs

141–142 **or it will...ruin** before it is ruined beyond repair

143 **doth commend** recommends

145 **he attendeth...by** he is waiting just outside

148 **give him...conduct** lead him politely

152 **in loving visitation** on a friendly visit

154 **cause in controversy** the case being argued about

156 **he is furnished with** he has been told

157 **bettered** improved

159 **importunity** request

to fill...stead to take my place in doing what your grace wants

160–161 **I beseech...estimation** I beg you, do not fail to judge his abilities respectfully, just because he is young

163–164 **whose trial...commendation** and the test you put him through will show his ability better than these words can

	Governed a wolf, who, hanged for human slaughter,	
	Even from the gallows did his fell soul fleet,	135
	And, whilst thou layest in thy unhallowed dam,	
	Infused itself in thee; for thy desires	
	Are wolvish, bloody, starved, and ravenous.	

SHYLOCK   Till thou canst rail the seal from off my bond,
             Thou but offend'st thy lungs to speak so loud;   140
             Repair thy wit, good youth, or it will fall
             To cureless ruin. I stand here for law.

DUKE   This letter from Bellario doth commend
             A young and learned doctor to our court.
             Where is he?

NERISSA   He attendeth here hard by   145
             To know your answer, whether you'll admit him.

DUKE   With all my heart; some three or four of you
             Go give him courteous conduct to this place;
             Meantime the court shall hear Bellario's letter.
             (*Reads*) *Your grace shall understand that at the receipt* 150
             of your letter I am very sick, but in the instant that your
             messenger came, in loving visitation was with me a
             young doctor of Rome; his name is Balthazar. I
             acquainted him with the cause in controversy between
             the Jew and Antonio the merchant; we turned o'er   155
             many books together; he is furnished with my opinion,
             which, bettered with his own learning, the greatness
             whereof I cannot enough commend, comes with him at
             my importunity, to fill up your grace's request in my
             stead. I beseech you let his lack of years be no   160
             impediment to let him lack a reverend estimation, for I
             never knew so young a body with so old a head. I
             leave him to your gracious acceptance, whose trial shall
             better publish his commendation.

Enter PORTIA, *dressed as* BALTHAZAR, *a doctor of laws.*

             You hear the learn'd Bellario what he writes,   165
             (*He sees* PORTIA) And here, I take it, is the doctor
                 come.
             (*To* PORTIA) Give me your hand. Came you from old
                 Bellario?

4.1 Venice: the Duke's palace

Portia opens the case by asking Shylock to be merciful. She explains the true nature of mercy and its power to soften the harshness of stark justice.

Activities

Actors' interpretations: 'Which is the merchant here...?'

Why is Portia unable to pick out Shylock in the court? Philip Voss pointed out that, in productions where Shylock and Antonio look very different, this question (line 170) can often make the audience laugh; and he felt that Shylock was wealthy and ought to be dressed like the rich merchants. What are the advantages and disadvantages of (a) dressing the two men similarly; (b) distinguishing them in their clothing, hair, etc?

Shakespeare's language: 'must'

PORTIA   Then must the Jew be merciful.
SHYLOCK On what compulsion must I? Tell me that.
(lines 180–181)

In this exchange, Portia's 'must' means that Shylock *ought* to be merciful, as it is the morally right thing to do; but Shylock interprets 'must' differently, and asks 'Who's going to force me?'

Act out the exchange bringing out the two different meanings. What differences will there be between the two characters' tones of voice?

169–170 **Are you...question?** are you familiar with the dispute being debated?

171 **throughly** thoroughly

175 **the suit you follow** the case you have brought

176–177 **in such rule...proceed** you have followed the rules so correctly that the law of Venice cannot oppose you if you pursue the case

178 **within his danger** at his mercy

181 **On what compulsion must I?** what is there that can make me?

182 **strained** forced; *you cannot force someone to be merciful*

186 **'Tis mightiest...** mercy is at its most powerful when powerful people show it

  becomes suits

188–189 **His sceptre...majesty** a king's sceptre (*staff of office*) is a symbol of his earthly (**temporal**) power, and the respect due to a king

191 **sway** rule

193 **an attribute to God** one of God's qualities

194 **doth...show likest** most closely resembles

195 **seasons** softens; tempers

PORTIA	I did, my lord.
DUKE	You are welcome; take your place; Are you acquainted with the difference That holds this present question in the court? 170
PORTIA	I am informèd throughly of the cause. Which is the merchant here? and which the Jew?
DUKE	Antonio and old Shylock, both stand forth.
PORTIA	Is your name Shylock?
SHYLOCK	Shylock is my name.
PORTIA	Of a strange nature is the suit you follow, 175 Yet in such rule that the Venetian law Cannot impugn you as you do proceed. (*To* ANTONIO) You stand within his danger, do you not?
ANTONIO	Ay, so he says.
PORTIA	Do you confess the bond?
ANTONIO	I do.
PORTIA	Then must the Jew be merciful. 180
SHYLOCK	On what compulsion must I? Tell me that.
PORTIA	The quality of mercy is not strained; It droppeth as the gentle rain from heaven Upon the place beneath; it is twice blest: It blesseth him that gives, and him that takes; 185 'T is mightiest in the mightiest; it becomes The thronèd monarch better than his crown. His sceptre shows the force of temporal power, The attribute to awe and majesty, Wherein doth sit the dread and fear of kings; 190 But mercy is above this sceptred sway; It is enthronèd in the hearts of kings; It is an attribute to God himself; And earthly power doth then show likest God's When mercy seasons justice. Therefore, Jew, 195

4.1 Venice: the Duke's palace

Portia argues that mercy is the only thing that can save people from damnation; but Shylock refuses to budge. When Bassanio asks the Duke to bend the law to save Antonio, Portia objects, saying that it would have a bad effect on future cases; and Shylock praises her wisdom and skill as a lawyer.

Activities

Themes: justice and mercy (2)

Portia's famous speech about mercy can be divided up into connected points. If she had been giving her speech at a debate, she might have written the following notes on her cue-card:
- lines 182–184: Giving mercy freely
- lines 184–185: Giving and receiving mercy
- lines 186–192: Kings and mercy
- lines 193: God and mercy
- lines 194–195: Justice and mercy
- lines 195–198: Mercy and salvation
- lines 198–200: Mercy and prayer.

Imagine you are the journalist from *The Rialto*. Write a report of Portia's speech in your own words, under the headline 'Balthazar mercy plea at Antonio trial'.

Portia (Marjorie Bland) and Shylock (Patrick Stewart) in the RSC 2978 production

197–198 in the course...salvation none of us would be saved from damnation if we had to depend solely upon justice

201 mitigate...plea soften that part of your plea which asks for pure justice

203 Must needs will have to

204 My deeds...head! I will accept the consequences of my actions

crave desire

206 discharge pay back

207 tender offer

212 malice...truth hatred is defeating what is right

213 Wrest...authority use your official power to bend the law

214 a little wrong *i.e. bending the law to defeat Shylock*

215 curb restrain; hold back

217 decree establishèd *a law which already exists*

218 a precedent *an example when judging similar future cases*

219–220 many an error...state many mistakes will be made, following the example of this case

221 a Daniel *Like Portia, Daniel in the Bible was young and gave a fair and just judgement.*

227 perjury lying under oath

228 bond is forfeit *in other words, Antonio has to pay the penalty*

Though justice be thy plea, consider this:
That in the course of justice none of us
Should see salvation; we do pray for mercy,
And that same prayer doth teach us all to render
The deeds of mercy. I have spoke thus much   200
To mitigate the justice of thy plea,
Which, if thou follow, this strict court of Venice
Must needs give sentence 'gainst the merchant
    there.

SHYLOCK   My deeds upon my head! I crave the law,
The penalty and forfeit of my bond.   205

PORTIA   Is he not able to discharge the money?

BASSANIO   Yes, here I tender it for him in the court;
Yea, twice the sum; if that will not suffice,
I will be bound to pay it ten times o'er
On forfeit of my hands, my head, my heart;   210
If this will not suffice, it must appear
That malice bears down truth. And I beseech you
Wrest once the law to your authority;
To do a great right, do a little wrong,
And curb this cruel devil of his will.   215

PORTIA   It must not be; there is no power in Venice
Can alter a decree establishèd;
'T will be recorded for a precedent,
And many an error by the same example
Will rush into the state. It cannot be: 220

SHYLOCK   A Daniel come to judgement! yea, a Daniel!
O wise young judge, how I do honour thee!

PORTIA   I pray you let me look upon the bond.

SHYLOCK   Here 't is, most reverend doctor, here it is.

PORTIA   Shylock, there's thrice thy money offered thee.   225

SHYLOCK   An oath, an oath, I have an oath in heaven –
Shall I lay perjury upon my soul?
No, not for Venice.

PORTIA   Why, this bond is forfeit,

4.1 Venice: the Duke's palace

Antonio takes a loving farewell of Bassanio, claiming to be glad that he will not have to live on in poverty and asking that Portia should be told about his love for Bassanio.

Activities

Character review: Antonio (5)

'I am armed and well prepared'

A What does Antonio say to Bassanio, when he realises he has definitely lost the case? Look back at his speech and complete the following statements:
- lines 264–270: Don't grieve about this, because…
- lines 271–275: Tell Portia…
- lines 275–279: If you're sorry to lose me…

B If you were directing the play, what advice would you give to the actor playing Antonio, about how to deliver this speech (lines 264–279)? Think about: tone of voice, gestures, facial expressions, pauses and movements.

C Look back at the activity on page 132. Then argue in groups about these two contrasting views of Antonio, using his speeches in this scene (lines 114–118 and 262–279) as evidence:
View A Antonio is generous and unselfish, willing to lay down his life for his friend.'
View B Antonio knows he has lost Bassanio to Portia and takes every opportunity to make Bassanio feel guilty and to demonstrate that he loves Bassanio more than Portia does.'

---

259 **'Twere good…charity** it would be a good thing to do out of human kindness

262 **armed** fortified in my mind; steeled

266 **still her use** always Fortune's usual way of doing things

269 **an age** an old age

ling'ring penance drawn-out punishment

272 **the process…end** how Antonio died

273 **speak me fair** say good things about me

276–277 **Repent but…debt** if you simply show that you are sorry to be losing me, I will not be sorry to pay this debt

283 **esteemed** valued

288 **protest** claim publicly

291 **'Tis well** it's just as well

292 **else** otherwise

| PORTIA | It is not so expressed, but what of that? |
| | 'T were good you do so much for charity. |

| SHYLOCK | I cannot find it; 't is not in the bond. | 260 |

| PORTIA | (*To* ANTONIO) You merchant, have you anything to say? |

ANTONIO But little, I am armed and well prepared.
Give me your hand, Bassanio; fare you well,
Grieve not that I am fall'n to this for you,
For herein Fortune shows herself more kind   265
Than is her custom. It is still her use
To let the wretched man outlive this wealth,
To view with hollow eye and wrinkled brow
An age of poverty: from which ling'ring penance
Of such misery doth she cut me off.   270
Commend me to your honourable wife;
Tell her the process of Antonio's end,
Say how I loved you, speak me fair in death;
And when the tale is told, bid her be judge
Whether Bassanio had not once a love;   275
Repent but you that you shall lose your friend
And he repents not that he pays your debt.
For if the Jew do cut but deep enough,
I'll pay it instantly, with all my heart.

BASSANIO Antonio, I am married to a wife   280
Which is as dear to me as life itself,
But life itself, my wife, and all the world,
Are not with me esteemed above thy life.
I would lose all, ay, sacrifice them all
Here to this devil, to deliver you.   285

| PORTIA | Your wife would give you little thanks for that |
| | If she were by to hear you make the offer. |

GRATIANO I have a wife who I protest I love –
I would she were in heaven, so she could
Entreat some power to change this currish Jew.   290

| NERISSA | 'T is well you offer it behind her back; |
| | The wish would make else an unquiet house. |

4.1 Venice: the Duke's palace

Portia adds a further condition: Shylock must take exactly a pound. Defeated, Shylock tries to leave, but Portia stops him with another law: if an 'alien' plots to kill a Venetian, half his wealth can be confiscated by the state and the other half given to the victim. He can also be executed.

Activities

Plot review (13): flesh and blood

Start drafting a front page for *The Rialto* to be published the day after the trial. Begin by writing the main article, in which you report the main events of the trial and its dramatic outcome (up to line 330). Include quotes from people present and give the article a dramatic headline.

Actors' interpretations: 'If it be proved against an alien...'

Some actors have noticed that Portia uses the word 'alien' when quoting the laws of Venice against Shylock. Patrick Stewart, who played Shylock in 1978, said '...when the word "alien" hits his ears he knows he is to be finished off. Once again he is an outsider, without rights and utterly vulnerable.'

Write a letter from Tubal to *The Rialto* about the unfair laws against aliens.

326–328 **in the substance...scruple** in the amount of a twentieth, or even the fraction of a twentieth

328 **scruple** a tiny quantity, used by chemists

332 **infidel** non-Christian (*see note to 3.2.217*)

on the hip at my mercy (*see note to 1.3.42*)

334 **my principal** the basic sum I lent him (*three thousand ducats*)

337 **merely** (1) only; (2) absolutely

340 **barely** only (*i.e. without interest added to it*)

344 **I'll stay...question** I'm not going to wait around to hear this case debated any further

347 **alien** foreigner (*not a citizen of Venice*)

350 **The party...contrive** the person he has plotted against

351 **seize** take possession of (*a legal term*)

4.1

GRATIANO	O Jew! an upright judge, a learned judge!
PORTIA	Therefore prepare thee to cut off the flesh;
	Shed thou no blood, nor cut thou less nor more
	But just a pound of flesh. If thou tak'st more
	Or less than a just pound, be it but so much 325
	As makes it light or heavy in the substance
	Or the division of the twentieth part
	Of one poor scruple – nay, if the scale do turn
	But in the estimation of a hair,
	Thou diest, and all thy goods are confiscate. 330
GRATIANO	A second Daniel, A Daniel, Jew!
	Now, infidel, I have you on the hip.
PORTIA	Why doth the Jew pause? (*To* SHYLOCK) Take thy
	forfeiture.
SHYLOCK	Give me my principal, and let me go.
BASSANIO	I have it ready for thee; here it is. 335
PORTIA	He hath refused it in the open court;
	He shall have merely justice and his bond.
GRATIANO	A Daniel still say I, a second Daniel!
	I thank thee Jew for teaching me that word.
SHYLOCK	Shall I not have barely my principal? 340
PORTIA	Thou shalt have nothing but the forfeiture,
	To be so taken at thy peril, Jew.
SHYLOCK	Why then, the devil give him good of it;
	I'll stay no longer question.
PORTIA	Tarry, Jew;
	The law hath yet another hold on you. 345
	It is enacted in the laws of Venice,
	If it be proved against an alien
	That by direct or indirect attempts
	He seek the life of any citizen,
	The party 'gainst the which he doth contrive, 350
	Shall seize one half his goods; the other half,

4.1 Venice: the Duke's palace

The Duke shows mercy: the state will not take half Shylock's money, but merely fine him. Antonio is willing to forget the fine, so long as he can have the other half of Shylock's wealth, to give to Lorenzo when Shylock dies. But there are two conditions: first, that Shylock must become a Christian.

Activities

Plot review (14): 'the law hath yet another hold…'

A The financial penalties imposed on Shylock are difficult to sort out. It helps to take the arrangements step-by-step.
- First re-read what happens, according to Portia, to aliens who have plotted against the life of a Venetian citizen (lines 350–355). What happens to their possessions?
- What does the Duke add to this (lines 368–370)? What will happen to Shylock's wealth according to him?
- What does Antonio propose doing with Shylock's wealth (lines 378–383)?

B Write an additional article for the front page of *The Rialto*, headed 'Further penalties on Shylock' and include the points Portia covers in lines 344–361. Then add details of the Duke's pardon (lines 366–370) and Antonio's conditions (lines 378–388).

C Talk together about the *financial* penalties imposed upon Shylock (lines 344–388). When looked at carefully, are they severe or lenient, in your view? What effect are they likely to have upon Shylock (a) financially, and (b) emotionally? What satisfaction can the Christians draw from them?

352 **privy coffer** the personal treasury of the Duke

354 **'gainst all other voice** without appeals (*i.e. the Duke has absolute power*)

355 **predicament** dangerous situation

356 **by manifest proceeding** by your clearly observed actions

359–360 **incurred…rehearsed** brought upon yourself the penalty that I have just described

364 **cord** rope (*to hang himself with*)

370 **Which humbleness…fine** if you behave humbly, you might be allowed to pay a fine instead of giving up half your wealth to the state

374 **That doth sustain** which supports

377 **halter gratis** hangman's rope, free of charge

379 **To quit** to release him from

380 **so he** so long as he

381 **in use** in trust (*not to employ in usury*)

381–383 **to render…daughter** *Antonio will hold on to half of Shylock's money (see line 366); when Shylock dies, this sum will go to Lorenzo.*

385 **presently** immediately

386 **record a gift** sign a legal 'deed of gift'; make a will

Comes to the privy coffer of the state,
And the offender's life lies in the mercy
Of the Duke only, 'gainst all other voice.
In which predicament I say thou stand'st;   355
For it appears by manifest proceeding,
That indirectly, and directly too,
Thou hast contrived against the very life
Of the defendant; and thou hast incurred
The danger formerly by me rehearsed.   360
Down, therefore, and beg mercy of the duke.

GRATIANO   Beg that thou may'st have leave to hang thyself.
And yet, thy wealth being forfeit to the state,
Thou hast not left the value of a cord;
Therefore thou must be hanged at the state's
    charge.   365

DUKE   That thou shalt see the difference of our spirit,
I pardon thee thy life before thou ask it;
For half thy wealth, it is Antonio's,
The other half comes to the general state,
Which humbleness may drive unto a fine.   370

PORTIA   Ay, for the state, not for Antonio.

SHYLOCK   Nay, take my life and all, pardon not that.
You take my house when you do take the prop
That doth sustain my house; you take my life
When you do take the means whereby I live.   375

PORTIA   What mercy can you render him, Antonio?

GRATIANO   A halter gratis; nothing else, for God's sake!

ANTONIO   So please my lord the Duke and all the court
To quit the fine for one half of his goods,
I am content; so he will let me have   380
The other half in use, to render it
Upon his death unto the gentleman
That lately stole his daughter.
Two things provided more: that for this favour
He presently become a Christian;   385
The other, that he do record a gift,

4.1 Venice: the Duke's palace

The second condition is that Shylock must agree to leave the rest of his wealth and any future earnings to Lorenzo after his death. Shylock agrees and leaves the court. The Duke thanks 'Balthazar' and Bassanio offers 'him' the three thousand ducats owed to Shylock.

Activities

Character review: Shylock (14)

'I am not well…'

Actors have taken different views about how Shylock should make his exit. Does he kick up a fuss or go gracefully? David Calder's Shylock (RSC, 1993) had a heart attack. Laurence Olivier's (1970) was heard to howl in anguish as he left the courtroom. Here are two other Shylocks:

- David Suchet (RSC, 1981): 'I don't personally go for the tense, anguished, howling kind of exit. My Shylock recognises that he has had a lucky escape and that the accommodation is a fair one. When he leaves the stage, he knows full well that he still has a life ahead of him.'
- Patrick Stewart (RSC, 1978): 'Gratiano makes a cruel joke out of Shylock's christening, and the person who must laugh most is, of course, Shylock. And so he leaves.'

Act out the moment in as many different ways as you can and decide which version fits your preferred interpretation of the character and the play as a whole.

387 **all he dies possessed** everything he owns at his death

388 **son** son-in-law

389 **recant** take back

390 **late** recently

396 **godfathers** (1) men named as a child's protector in a christening; (2) slang term for jurymen (*because they sent the condemned man to God*)

397 **ten more** *to bring the number up to the twelve required to sentence him to hang*

399 **entreat** beg

400 **of pardon** to excuse me

402 **it is meet…forth** and it is fitting that I leave immediately

403 **your leisure serves you not** you don't have the time

404 **gratify** reward

405 **are much bound to him** owe him a great deal

407 **acquitted Of** released from

408 **in lieu whereof** in return for which

409–410 **Three thousand…withal** we willingly give you the three thousand ducats owed to Shylock, as recompense for your great efforts

4.1

Here in the court, of all he dies possessed
Unto his son Lorenzo and his daughter.

DUKE   He shall do this, or else I do recant
         The pardon that I late pronouncèd here.   390

PORTIA   Art thou contented, Jew? What dost thou say?

SHYLOCK   I am content.

PORTIA   Clerk, draw a deed of gift.

SHYLOCK   I pray you give me leave to go from hence;
         I am not well; send the deed after me,
         And I will sign it.

DUKE   Get thee gone, but do it.   395

GRATIANO   In christening shalt thou have two godfathers;
         Had I been judge, thou shouldst have had ten
              more,
         To bring thee to the gallows, not to the font.

                                        Exit SHYLOCK.

DUKE   Sir, I entreat you home with me to dinner.

PORTIA   I humbly do desire your grace of pardon;   400
         I must away this night toward Padua,
         And it is meet I presently set forth.

DUKE   I am sorry that your leisure serves you not.
         Antonio, gratify this gentlemen,
         For in my mind you are much bound to him.   405

                                Exit DUKE *and his train.*

BASSANIO   Most worthy gentleman, I and my friend
         Have by your wisdom been this day acquitted
         Of grievous penalties, in lieu whereof,
         Three thousand ducats due unto the Jew
         We freely cope your courteous pains withal.   410

ANTONIO   And stand indebted over and above
         In love and service to you evermore.

4.2 Near the Duke's palace

Antonio persuades Bassanio to give the ring to the young lawyer and Bassanio reluctantly sends Gratiano in pursuit. Out in the street, Portia politely accepts the gift and Nerissa decides to test Gratiano, by seeing if she can get her ring off him.

Activities

Actors' interpretations: the ring

1. Do you think Bassanio was right to give up the ring? List the arguments for and against. Decide what you would have done in his position.

2. If you were directing a production of the play, what advice would you give the actor playing Gratiano about how he should react when Bassanio tells him to run after the lawyer and give him the ring (4.1.450–452)? Should he hesitate, appalled, as some actors do, for example?

   Write down Gratiano's thoughts as he sets off after the lawyer.

3. What advice would you give the actress playing Portia when she receives the ring from Gratiano (4.2.5–11)? Should she be amused, or deeply hurt, for example?

   Write down her thoughts and emotions concerning the ring, as she leaves Venice. Include her thoughts on why she asked for the ring in the first place.

---

448 **withal** as well

455 **Fly** hasten

1 **Inquire...out** find out where Shylock lives

 this deed *i.e. the deed of gift (see 4.1.384–386)*

5 **you are well o'erta'en** I'm glad I've caught up with you

6 **upon more advice** after further thought

7 **entreat** beg

ANTONIO	My Lord Bassanio, let him have the ring;
	Let his deservings and my love withal
	Be valued 'gainst your wife's commandement.

BASSANIO	Go, Gratiano, run and overtake him,	450
	Give him the ring, and bring him if thou canst
	Unto Antonio's house. Away, make haste.

Exit GRATIANO.

Come, you and I will thither presently,
And in the morning early will we both
Fly toward Belmont. Come, Antonio.   455

Exeunt.

Scene 2

Venice. A street.

Enter PORTIA *and* NERISSA.

PORTIA   Inquire the Jew's house out; give him this deed,
And let him sign it. We'll away to-night,
And be a day before our husbands home.
This deed will be well welcome to Lorenzo!

Enter GRATIANO.

GRATIANO   Fair sir, you are well o'erta'en: 5
My Lord Bassanio, upon more advice
Hath sent you here this ring, and doth entreat
Your company at dinner.

PORTIA   That cannot be;
His ring I do accept most thankfully,
And so I pray you tell him. Furthermore,   10
I pray you show my youth old Shylock's house.

GRATIANO   That will I do.

NERISSA   Sir, I would speak with you.
(*Aside to* PORTIA) I'll see if I can get my husband's
    ring,
Which I did make him swear to keep for ever.

4.2 Near the Duke's palace

Portia and Nerissa predict that the men will have a hard time convincing them that they didn't give the rings away to other women!

Activities

Actors' interpretations: 4.2 – comic or serious?

Re-read the activity on page 154. Then talk together about whether 4.2 ought to be played light-heartedly (perhaps as a contrast to the trial), or more seriously (to bring out the importance of Bassanio's act in giving away the ring).

Character review: Nerissa (3)

What part has Nerissa played, since she arrived in Venice with Portia? Write another entry in her diary, in which she records her part in the trial (including any preparations she and Portia made beforehand) and what happened after the trial.

15 **Thou may'st, I warrant** I bet you will

old swearing plenty of swearing (oath-taking)

17 **outface them** boldly stand our ground and shame them

18 **tarry** wait

PORTIA Thou may'st, I warrant. We shall have old
            swearing   15
        That they did give the rings away to men;
        But we'll outface them, and outswear them too.
        Away, make haste! Thou know'st where I will tarry.

NERISSA Come, good sir, will you show me to this house?

Exeunt.

5.1 Belmont: Portia's garden

In Belmont Lorenzo and Jessica are recalling lovers from classical mythology who met on moonlit nights such as this one, when Stephano, one of Portia's servants, arrives.

Activities

Themes: love (2)

As they sit in the moonlight, Lorenzo and Jessica recall legendary lovers:

- Troilus (line 4), son of King Priam of Troy, was in love with Cressida; Shakespeare's play *Troilus and Cressida* tells how the lovers are parted when Cressida is taken over to the enemy Greek camp
- Thisbe (line 7) is the tragic heroine of the play put on by the Athenian workmen at the end of Shakespeare's *A Midsummer Night's Dream*; she flees from a lion and later kills herself after discovering the body of her lover, Pyramus
- Dido (line 10) was the Queen of Carthage, deserted by her lover Æneas
- Medea (line 13) was abandoned by Jason, having helped him win the Golden Fleece. Medea used a magic herbal brew to make her father Æson (line 14) young again.

Re-read lines 1–22 in pairs, first as though Lorenzo and Jessica are happily in love and enjoying the moonlight; then as though they are reminding each other about all the past lovers who have been deserted and made unhappy (suggesting that they themselves will not have a happy marriage). Which version fits your interpretation of the play?

7 **o'ertrip** step lightly across

10 **willow** *an emblem of forsaken love*

11 **waft** wave to

12 **again** back

15 **steal** (1) creep away; (2) thieve

16 **unthrift** unthrifty; like a spendthrift

19 **vows** promises

21 **shrew** *someone who nags*

22 **Slander** criticise unfairly

23 **out-night you** out-do you in telling stories which begin 'In such a night'

24 **footing** footsteps

Act 5

Scene 1

Belmont. A green place in front of Portia's house. Night-time.

Enter LORENZO *and* JESSICA.

LORENZO   The moon shines bright. In such a night as this,
When the sweet wind did gently kiss the trees,
And they did make no noise, in such a night
Troilus methinks mounted the Trojan walls,
And sighed his soul toward the Grecian tents   5
Where Cressid lay that night.

JESSICA   In such a night
Did Thisbe fearfully o'ertrip the dew,
And saw the lion's shadow ere himself,
And ran dismayed away.

LORENZO   In such a night
Stood Dido with a willow in her hand   10
Upon the wild sea banks, and waft her love
To come again to Carthage.

JESSICA   In such a night
Medea gathered the enchanted herbs
That did renew old Æson.

LORENZO   In such a night
Did Jessica steal from the wealthy Jew,   15
And with an unthrift love did run from Venice
As far as Belmont.

JESSICA   In such a night
Did young Lorenzo swear he loved her well,
Stealing her soul with many vows of faith,
And ne'er a true one.

LORENZO   In such a night   20
Did pretty Jessica, like a little shrew,
Slander her love, and he forgave it her.

JESSICA   I would out-night you did nobody come:
But hark, I hear the footing of a man.

Enter STEPHANO.

5.1 Belmont: Portia's garden

Stephano reports that Portia is expected home before dawn and Launcelot enters to say that a messenger has brought news that Bassanio will be back at the same time.

Activities

Actors' interpretations: 'In such a night...'

Look back at the activity on page 150. What can you tell about Lorenzo and Jessica from this scene from the 1997 RSC production? Which word would you chose to describe their mood (romantic; sad; wistful...)? How does the set design help to create the atmosphere?

Emma Handy and Dominic Rowan as Jessica and Lorenzo (RSC 1997)

30–31 **stray...crosses** she stops occasionally by wayside shrines

32 **wedlock** marriage

33 **hermit** *holy man who lives alone*

37–38 **ceremoniously...welcome** arrange some ceremony to welcome

39 **Sola...!** *Launcelot imitates the sound of a messenger's post-horn.*

43 **Leave hollowing** stop shouting

46 **a post** a messenger

47 **horn** (1) his post-horn; (2) *a reminder of the 'horn of plenty', full of good things*

49 **expect** await

LORENZO	Who comes so fast in silence of the night?	25
STEPHANO	A friend!	
LORENZO	A friend! what friend? your name, I pray you, friend?	
STEPHANO	Stephano is my name, and I bring word My mistress will before the break of day Be here at Belmont. She doth stray about By holy crosses, where she kneels and prays For happy wedlock hours.	30
LORENZO	Who comes with her?	
STEPHANO	None but a holy hermit and her maid. I pray you, is my master yet returned?	
LORENZO	He is not, nor we have not heard from him. But go we in, I pray thee, Jessica, And ceremoniously let us prepare Some welcome for the mistress of the house.	35

Enter LAUNCELOT.

LAUNCELOT	Sola, sola, wo ha, ho! sola, sola!	
LORENZO	Who calls?	40
LAUNCELOT	Sola! did you see Master Lorenzo? Master Lorenzo, sola, sola!	
LORENZO	Leave hollowing man; here!	
LAUNCELOT	Sola! where, where?	
LORENZO	Here!	45
LAUNCELOT	Tell him there's a post come from my master, with his horn full of good news; my master will be here ere morning.	

Exit.

LORENZO	Sweet soul, let's in, and there expect their coming. And yet no matter; why should we go in?	50

5.1 Belmont: Portia's garden

As Portia and Nerissa approach they see the light shining from the house and hear the music. Lorenzo recognises Portia's voice and welcomes her back.

Activities

Shakespeare's language: music

When Jessica says that she is never merry when she hears sweet music, Lorenzo's explanation includes references to wild animals, the mythological Orpheus, and treacherous plotters (lines 69–88). Create a collage which represents every element of his speech and include some of your favourite lines. You will be able to find most of the images that you need in magazines, but the collage will probably require some additional drawing of your own. Given that the speech is about music, try to find a piece which could be played as people look at your collage.

Portia (Derbhla Crotty) and Nerissa (Alex Kelly) in the 1999 RNT production

84 **concord** peaceful harmony

85 **strategems** plotting violent deeds

spoils destruction

86 **motions of his spirit** the impulses of his mind; his sensitivity

87 **affections** thoughts and feelings

Erebus *a region of darkness in the classical underworld*

88 **Mark** listen to

91 **naughty** wicked (*see 3.3.9*)

95–97 **his state…waters** the substitute king's dignity disappears like a stream's waters flowing into the sea

99 **without respect** until it is compared with something else

101 **bestows that virtue** gives it that power (*of sounding sweeter*)

103 **attended** (1) listened to; (2) accompanied by other birds

107–108 **How many…perfection!** how many things are only at their best if they are enjoyed at particular times

109 **Endymion** *a young shepherd in Greek mythology, loved by the moon goddess, Diana; to preserve his youth and beauty, she caused him to sleep for ever*

Nor is not moved with concord of sweet sounds,
Is fit for treasons, stratagems, and spoils;   85
The motions of his spirit are dull as night,
And his affections dark as Erebus;
Let no such man be trusted. Mark the music.

Enter PORTIA *and* NERISSA, *at a distance from the others.*

PORTIA   That light we see is burning in my hall.
How far that little candle throws his beams!   90
So shines a good deed in a naughty world.

NERISSA   When the moon shone, we did not see the candle.

PORTIA   So doth the greater glory dim the less;
A substitute shines brightly as a king
Until a king be by, and then his state   95
Empties itself, as doth an inland brook
Into the main of waters – Music! hark!

NERISSA   It is your music, madam, of the house.

PORTIA   Nothing is good, I see, without respect;
Methinks it sounds much sweeter than by day.   100

NERISSA   Silence bestows that virtue on it, madam.

PORTIA   The crow doth sing as sweetly as the lark
When neither is attended; and I think
The nightingale, if she should sing by day,
When every goose is cackling, would be thought   105
No better a musician than the wren!
How many things by season seasoned are
To their right praise, and true perfection!
Peace! – how the moon sleeps with Endymion,
And would not be awaked!

Music ceases.

LORENZO   That is the voice,   110
Or I am much deceived, of Portia.

PORTIA   He knows me as the blind man knows the cuckoo –
By the bad voice!

LORENZO   Dear lady, welcome home!

5.1 Belmont: Portia's garden

A quarrel breaks out between Nerissa and Gratiano: she accuses him of having given his ring away to a woman and refuses to believe his story that he gave it to the judge's clerk. Portia takes Nerissa's side, saying that Bassanio would never give her ring away!

Activities

Actors' interpretations

Imagine you are directing the play. Write notes for the actors in this part of the scene (lines 142–209), advising them on how they should act and react (especially when they are not speaking). For example:

- How does the argument between Nerissa and Gratiano break out (line 142)?
- How should Portia react (line 146), given that she probably knows what they are quarrelling about?
- How does Nerissa keep up the pretence of believing that Gratiano had given the ring to a woman (lines 151–158)?
- How does she react to being called 'a scrubbèd boy, No higher than thyself' (lines 162–163)?
- What does Bassanio do when Portia says:
  'I gave my love a ring, and made him swear
  Never to part with it, and here he stands' (lines 170–171)?
- How do Bassanio and Portia each react when Gratiano reveals, 'My lord Bassanio gave his ring away' (line 179)?

Continued on page 172

144 **Would he…part** as far as I'm concerned, I wish he were castrated (**gelt**)

147 **paltry** worthless

148 **posy** *motto inscribed on the inside of the ring*

149 **cutler's poetry** *rather poor verse inscribed on a knife-handle (these days we might refer scornfully to Christmas-cracker mottoes)*

155 **Though not…respective** you should have thought about the circumstances under which you received it, if not for my sake, then for the passionate promises you made

158 **The clerk…had it** the clerk who had the ring will never have a beard

162 **scrubbèd** stunted (*low-growing bushes are called 'scrub'*)

164 **prating** nattering, over-talkative

169 **riveted** immovably fixed

174 **masters** possesses

176 **An 't were to me** if it had happened to me

GRATIANO	(*To* NERISSA) By yonder moon I swear you do me	
	wrong;	
	In faith I gave it to the judge's clerk	
	Would he were gelt that had it for my part,	
	Since you do take it, love, so much at heart.	145

PORTIA   A quarrel, ho, already! What's the matter?

GRATIANO About a hoop of gold, a paltry ring
That she did give me, whose posy was
For all the world like cutler's poetry
Upon a knife: "Love me, and leave me not."   150

NERISSA What talk you of the posy or the value?
You swore to me when I did give it you
That you would wear it till your hour of death,
And that it should lie with you in your grave.
Though not for me, yet for your vehement oaths   155
You should have been respective and have kept it.
Gave it a judge's clerk! No, God's my judge,
The clerk will ne'er wear hair on's face that had it.

GRATIANO He will, and if he live to be a man.

NERISSA Ay, if a woman live to be a man.   160

GRATIANO Now, by this hand, I gave it to a youth,
A kind of boy, a little scrubbèd boy,
No higher than thyself, the judge's clerk,
A prating boy that begged it as a fee.
I could not for my heart deny it him.   165

PORTIA You were to blame, I must be plain with you,
To part so slightly with your wife's first gift,
A thing stuck on with oaths upon your finger,
And so riveted with faith unto your flesh.
I gave my love a ring, and made him swear   170
Never to part with it, and here he stands.
I dare be sworn for him he would not leave it,
Nor pluck it from his finger, for the wealth
That the world masters. Now, in faith, Gratiano,
You give your wife too unkind a cause of grief;   175
An 't were to me I should be mad at it.

5.1 Belmont: Portia's garden

Bassanio tries in vain to explain why he felt obliged to give the ring to the young lawyer, but Portia and Nerissa threaten to have sex with the lawyer and his clerk if ever they visit Belmont.

Activities

Character review: Antonio (7)

'I am th'unhappy subject of these quarrels'

Write the entry in Antonio's diary which records his experiences from the moment he arrives in Belmont up to the argument which breaks out between Portia and Bassanio (lines 127–238). You might include his recollections of:

- his arrival in Belmont (what did he think of Portia when she first welcomed him?)
- the way the quarrel broke out between Gratiano and Nerissa
- Bassanio's admission that he had given away his ring too
- Portia's reactions.

He says nothing once the lovers start quarrelling until line 238. What goes through his mind?

Shakespeare's language: dramatic irony (2)

Talk together about the dramatic irony in lines 223–235. What exactly does the audience know, that Bassanio and Gratiano do not know?

---

210 **civil doctor** *lawyer specialising in citizen's rights (civil law)*

213 **suffered** caused

214 **held up** preserved

217 **I was beset...courtesy** I was overcome by shame; I had to show good manners

219 **besmear** spoil

220 **blessèd candles** the stars

226 **liberal** (1) generous; (2) free with my body

229 **Know him** (1) recognise; (2) have sex with (*see 4.1.415 and the activity on page 152*)

230 **Lie not...home** don't sleep a single night away from home

   Argus *a giant in Greek mythology; only two of his hundred eyes slept at any one time*

232 **mine honour...own** she is still a virgin

233 **I'll have...bedfellow** I'll sleep with that lawyer!

234–235 **be well advised...** think carefully before leaving me to my own devices!

236 **take** catch

237 **mar** spoil

   pen *with a bawdy meaning of 'penis'*

239 **notwithstanding** despite everything else (*the quarrels*)

243 **Mark you but that** just listen to that!

	No woman had it, but a civil doctor,	210
	Which did refuse three thousand ducats of me,	
	And begged the ring; the which I did deny him,	
	And suffered him to go displeased away,	
	Even he that had held up the very life	
	Of my dear friend. What should I say, sweet lady?	215
	I was enforced to send it after him;	
	I was beset with shame and courtesy;	
	My honour would not let ingratitude	
	So much besmear it. Pardon me, good lady,	
	For by these blessèd candles of the night,	220
	Had you been there, I think you would have begged	
	The ring of me to give the worthy doctor.	

PORTIA   Let not that doctor e'er come near my house.
Since he hath got the jewel that I loved,
And that which you did swear to keep for me,   225
I will become as liberal as you;
I'll not deny him anything I have,
No, not my body, nor my husband's bed;
Know him I shall, I am well sure of it.
Lie not a night from home. Watch me like Argus;   230
If you do not, if I be left alone,
Now by mine honour, which is yet mine own,
I'll have that doctor for my bedfellow.

NERISSA   And I his clerk; therefore be well advised
How you do leave me to mine own protection.   235

GRATIANO   Well, do you so; let not me take him then,
For if I do, I'll mar the young clerk's pen.

ANTONIO   I am th' unhappy subject of these quarrels.

PORTIA   Sir, grieve not you; you are welcome
notwithstanding.

BASSANIO   Portia, forgive me this enforcèd wrong,   240
And, in the hearing of these many friends,
I swear to thee, even by thine own fair eyes,
Wherein I see myself –

PORTIA   Mark you but that
In both my eyes he doubly sees himself;

5.1 Belmont: Portia's garden

In the general amazement, Portia hands Lorenzo the document which gives him all Shylock's wealth on his death. They go indoors to hear the full story from Portia.

Activities

Plot review (19): answering Portia's questions

At the end of some mystery films, the main characters sit down with the detective and somebody says, 'But there's one thing I don't understand...'

In this play, Portia invites everyone into the house and promises to 'answer all things faithfully' (line 299). Draw up a list of the questions that each character might put to her, and then write down her replies.

Pippa Guard as Nerissa and Geoffrey Freshwater as Gratiano (seated), with Deborah Findlay as Portia, Nicholas Farrell as Bassanio, Deborah Goodman as Jessica and Paul Spence as Lorenzo (RSC 1987)

279 **chancèd on** came upon by chance

I am dumb! I am lost for words!

286 **living** livelihood; his means of living

288 **come to road** anchored

292 **deed of gift** *see 4.1.384–386*

293 **dies possessed of** possesses when he dies

294 **manna** *in the Bible, the miraculous food which came from heaven to sustain the Israelites in the desert*

295 **starvèd people** *Lorenzo and Jessica have possibly spent all the money stolen from Shylock (see 3.1.102–106, for example).*

296–297 **you are not...full** you do not yet know all you want to about these events

298 **charge...inter'gatories** we will answer as though we were being examined under oath; *legal jargon: people in court are instructed (**charged**) on oath to answer specific questions (**inter'gatories**)*

302 **she had rather stay** she would prefer to wait

305 **couching** in bed

307 **So sore** so strongly

ring *a bawdy pun: 'ring' can mean the vulva*

You shall not know by what strange accident
I chancèd on this letter.

ANTONIO   I am dumb!

BASSANIO   Were you the doctor, and I knew you not?   280

GRATIANO   Were you the clerk that is to make me cuckold?

NERISSA   Ay, but the clerk that never means to do it,
Unless he live until he be a man.

BASSANIO   Sweet doctor, you shall be my bedfellow;
When I am absent then lie with my wife.   285

ANTONIO   Sweet lady, you have given me life and living;
For here I read for certain that my ships
Are safely come to road.

PORTIA   How now, Lorenzo?
My clerk hath some good comforts too for you.

NERISSA   Ay, and I'll give them him without a fee.   290
There do I give to you and Jessica,
From the rich Jew, a special deed of gift,
After his death, of all he dies possessed of.

LORENZO   Fair ladies, you drop manna in the way
Of starvèd people.

PORTIA   It is almost morning,   295
And yet I am sure you are not satisfied
Of these events at full. Let us go in,
And charge us there upon inter'gatories,
And we will answer all things faithfully.

GRATIANO   Let it be so; the first inter'gatory   300
That my Nerissa shall be sworn on is,
Whether till the next night she had rather stay,
Or go to bed now, being two hours to day;
But were the day come, I should wish it dark
Till I were couching with the doctor's clerk.   305
Well, while I live I'll fear no other thing
So sore as keeping safe Nerissa's ring.

Exeunt.

Exam practice

Character review: Portia (7)

In 5.1 Portia returns from Venice and confronts Bassanio with the loss of her ring. Comment in detail on the different ways in which she seems to punish Bassanio for having given the ring away.

Before you write, you should think about:
- the way she supports Nerissa's complaint against Gratiano, when he admits to having given his ring away
- her reaction when Gratiano reveals that Bassanio has given away his ring
- her response to Bassanio's excuses
- the way she keeps up the pretence of believing that the ring had been given to a woman
- her claim to have slept with the doctor.

Actors' interpretations: the ending

A Create a freeze-frame to represent the final moment of the play. First discuss how each character might be feeling as Gratiano speaks the concluding lines. What is Jessica thinking and feeling, for example? Should Shylock be represented in the freeze-frame?

B Although Shakespeare's script seems to end on a light note, some productions of the play have reminded us that there are a number of characters who might not be able to join in with the jollity. Here are five different endings from actual productions. Act out each one and then talk about the different effects that each might have on the audience:
- RSC, 1987: Jessica has been wearing a cross, to show that she has become a Christian. As she leaves, she drops it and returns to retrieve it. But Antonio gets there first. He picks it up and offers it to Jessica; but, instead of handing it over, dangles it in front of her, as the lights dim.
- English Shakespeare Company, 1990: The play is set in the 1930s. As Gratiano delivers the final couplet, the band strikes up and the couples begin to dance. After a few moments, Antonio approaches Portia and Bassanio and taps Bassanio on the shoulder, as people do in an 'excuse-me', where you are allowed to take someone else's partner. The couple break apart, smilingly, and Antonio begins to dance – with Bassanio!
- National Theatre, 1970: The final scene has taken place outside Portia's house; as they enter, we hear the sound of a Jewish hymn of sadness and lament.
- Compass Theatre, 1997: This scene also took place outside Portia's house. At the end, Jessica was the last to leave and, as she approached the door, Antonio shut it in her face.
- Wheatley Productions, 1990: The play ended exactly as it had begun: with Antonio, sitting alone, taking a hip-flask out of his pocket and drinking.

C Why do you think Shakespeare:
- gives the concluding lines to Gratiano?
- ends the play with a bawdy pun?

What effect does that have on your interpretation of the play as a whole?

Write down your opinions of (a) Shakespeare's ending; and (b) the alternatives described in **B** above (and any other endings that you might have seen). How would you conclude the play?

Plot review (20): the strands chart

Complete the chart (see the activity on page 80) which shows how the three strands are connected. In particular, look at the way Shakespeare continues to make connections with the Shylock–Antonio strand in Act 5, even though Shylock's last appearance in the script is towards the end of 4.1.

Plot review (21): a time-line

Draw up a time-line of the play to show when the main events happened. You might find it helpful to have three parallel lines, based on the three plot-strands (see page 80). The bond signed by Antonio (see 1.3.2) gives you one major piece of information about how much time passes in this story.

Henry Goodman as Shylock in the 1999 RNT production

Activities

Thinking about the play as a whole . . .

Actor's interpretations

1   **A**   *Filming the play*

Pick your favourite scene from the play and draw a sketch to show what a key moment might look like, adding notes to explain details of the characters' actions, expressions and gestures. You might pick Shylock sharpening his knife, for example, or one of the suitors choosing a casket.

B   *Staging scenes*

Pick two contrasting moments from the play (for example, Launcelot Gobbo's tricking of his father and Portia's speech about mercy at the trial) and, using the outline or plan on page 199, show how the moments might be staged to bring out the contrasts, writing annotations to explain your decisions.

C   *Directing an extract*

Annotate a short scene or extract to show actors' movements, actions and reactions. Introduce it with a statement about the particular interpretation that you are aiming for (such as a portrayal of Shylock as a loving father).

2   **A**   *Casting the play*

If you had the chance to direct a performance of *The Merchant of Venice* on stage, which actors and actresses would you cast in the various roles? Make decisions about each character, explaining why you think the particular performer would be right for the part.

B   *A theatre programme*

Create a theatre programme for a production of *The Merchant of Venice*. This might include:
- a cast list with the names of the actors
- some background material (for example, about anti-Semitism – see pages 200–202; or articles on the language or some of the major themes)
- details about Shakespeare and his plays (see pages 214–216).

C *A modern film adaptation*

Write your own review of *The Merchant of Venice*, as a response to an actual theatre performance, or any one of the video versions that you have seen.

3 *Film versions*

The best known versions of *The Merchant of Venice* on video are those of the National Theatre (1973), the BBC (1980) and Channel 4 (1996).

In groups, think up some ideas for a modern film adaptation of *The Merchant of Venice* (possibly on the lines of Baz Luhrmann's *Romeo + Juliet*:
(a) Make decisions about actors to play the roles and locations for the different scenes of the story.
(b) Storyboard one of the key sequences and bring out the special qualities of your new interpretation.
(c) Discuss which features of the play (not only the story, but its themes and language) you would hope to bring out most successfully and which would be harder to get across.

4 **A** *An advertisement*

Create a poster or magazine advert for a new production of *The Merchant of Venice*, featuring some of your favourite actors. First look at some examples in magazines, to see how images are used and what written material is included.

B *Video covers*

Discuss the two covers of video versions of *The Merchant of Venice* shown on page 184.
• Which features of the story do they seem to be concentrating on? What 'image' is each one conveying? In what ways will the interpretations be different?
• Which characters have they decided to highlight?
• How have they arranged the images?
• What text have they used to 'sell' the product?

Create a video cover for your own screen production of the play (which might feature some of the performers chosen for activity 3).

Activities

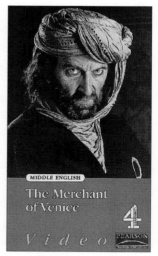

National Theatre, 1973

Channel 4, 1996

C *A display*

Put together a classroom display on *The Merchant of Venice*, which would be interesting for a younger class approaching the play for the first time.
Include:

- any drawings that you have done (staging designs, storyboards...)
- other background work (characters' letters and journal entries, the newspaper reports, the triptych, the Appearance and Reality poster, the time-chart...)
- anything else you can think of (a poster advertising the play; cartoons of images...)
- things that you have collected from productions (production postcards, programmes, reviews...).

You will need to write some introductory material, explaining what the play is about and how the various elements of the display tie in.

Character reviews

5 **Character profiles**

Many actors write systematic notes about the characters they are preparing to play. Draw up a CHARACTER PROFILE form on a word-processor and then fill it in for any characters you are working on. Headings might be:

NAME:

SOCIAL POSITION:

SUPER-OBJECTIVE: (the character's overriding aim, which drives them on, e.g. 'to win Portia')

LINE OF ACTION: (the practical things they must do to achieve that aim, e.g. 'pick the right casket')

OBSTACLES AGAINST IT: (e.g. 'there are three caskets, each with a riddling inscription')

WHAT THE CHARACTER SAYS ABOUT HERSELF/HIMSELF:

WHAT OTHER CHARACTERS SAY ABOUT HER/HIM:

IMPRESSION ON FIRST APPEARANCE:

RELATIONSHIPS WITH OTHERS:

OTHER INFORMATION:

6 Character review: Portia

Portia saves Antonio's life and displays many strong qualities. And yet many audiences do not have great affection for her. Look back at the following scenes: 1.2, 2.1, 2.7, 2.9, 3.2, 3.4, 4.1, 4.2 and 5.1.

A *Portia's qualities*

What would you say Portia's strongest qualities were? List as many as you can and find moments in the play to support each one. For example, can you find moments in the play where she displays some of the following: humour; perceptiveness; affection; cleverness; mercy; self-restraint; love; understanding; resourcefulness; loyalty?

B *Her own feelings*

Write a section for Portia's autobiography, in which she writes about her love for Bassanio, describes how she felt when he gave her ring away and explains why she decided to act as she did on their return to Belmont.

C *Contrasting views of Portia*

While many people admire Portia for her good qualities (see **A** above), others find her hard-hearted and cold, claiming that she manipulates Shylock in the trial and is then very hard on Bassanio for giving away the ring. What is your view? Write a newspaper article in praise of Portia for the weekend section of *The Rialto*, and then draft a letter sent in by a reader who takes an opposing view.

7 Character review: Shylock

Is Shylock a villain? Or a victim who deserves our sympathy? Look back at the following scenes: 1.3, 2.5, 2.8, 3.1, 3.3 and 4.1.

Activities

Ⓐ *His different faces*

Pick one scene in which Shylock appears. List (a) all the things which make you dislike him; and (b) the things which give you sympathy for him.

Ⓑ *Sympathy for him?*

Talk together about whether you feel that Shylock deserves what happens to him. Then draw a graph. On the x axis, mark at least ten points in the story of Shylock (including his first and last appearances). On the y axis, draw a scale of 0–10, according to how much sympathy you feel for him (10 being the highest). Plot your graph and then compare it with other people's, discussing the differences in your responses. Finally, write an essay entitled 'How much sympathy I feel for Shylock'.

Ⓒ *A great part to play*

What is there about the role of Shylock which has attracted so many famous actors over the centuries? Write a letter to someone who has been offered the chance to play the part, explaining why it would be a great experience. You might want to refer to the character's ambiguity (is he villain or victim?) and the range of comic and serious (even tragic?) moments.

8 Character review: Antonio

Antonio is 'the Merchant' referred to in the title; and yet there is much about him that remains puzzling. Look back at the following scenes: 1.1, 1.3, 2.6, 3.3, 4.1 and 5.1.

Ⓐ *His different faces*

What would you say were Antonio's good and bad points? (Look at his treatment of Bassanio and Shylock, for example.) Talk together about whether you admire him or not.

Ⓑ *His true feelings*

Imagine you are Antonio, alone in your cell the night before the trial. You do not know whether Bassanio has received your letter asking him to come to Venice, so you decide to write a final letter to him, explaining how you feel. Write the letter, but first think about:
- why you were so willing to agree to Shylock's bond
- how you feel about Bassanio's marriage to Portia
- what hope you have of escaping from Shylock's clutches.

Thinking about the play as a whole ...

C *Questions answered*

Why is Antonio 'so sad' at the beginning of the play? Why does he agree to a bond which looks so dangerous? What are his true feelings for Bassanio? Why has he treated Shylock so badly in the past? Why does he call himself a 'tainted wether'? How does he feel at the end of the play? Write an interview with Antonio for the weekend section of *The Rialto*, in which you have attempted to find answers to these and other questions.

9 **Character review: Bassanio**

Some people would call Bassanio the 'hero' of the play; but many do not find him attractive or appealing. Look back at the following scenes: 1.1, 1.3, 2.2, 3.2, 4.1 and 5.1.

A *Bassanio's attractions*

Which qualities of Bassanio make Portia fall in love with him, in your opinion? Look back at his conversations with Antonio and his friends in Acts 1 and 2, the way he behaves with Portia in Act 3, his words at the trial and his behaviour with the ring.

B *Descriptions of Bassanio*

Write two descriptions of Bassanio, one by Antonio, the other by Shylock. Concentrate particularly on the different sides of the man that each one sees.

C *Actors' interpretations*

Write an essay in which you discuss the different ways in which Bassanio can be played: as a carefree young lover; a spoiled rich boy; an irresponsible spendthrift; a man who has seen the error of his ways and is determined to reform... If you were directing the play, which interpretation would you aim to bring out, and which parts of the script would you focus on to support it?

10 **Character review: Launcelot Gobbo**

Launcelot can be hilarious in some productions of the play and extremely irritating in others. Look back at the following scenes: 2.2, 2.3, 2.4, 2.5, 3.5 and 5.1.

A *Launcelot's role*

What exactly does Launcelot do in the story? Look back through the play and draw a diagram or flow-chart which shows (a) what he actually does; and (b) how he is connected to the various characters.

Activities

(c) Look back at the activities on the theme of appearance and reality (pages 33, 48, 74, 125) and complete your wall-chart or poster. What are the best examples of 'things not being what they seem' in the play?

(d) The director John Barton said that *The Merchant of Venice* was about 'true and false values'. What do you think he meant? Which 'true values' turn out to be the most important to people in this play? Which characters fail because they rely too much on 'false values'? Do any characters learn about true and false values through their experiences in the play?

(e) How does the play present the relationship between Jews and Christians? What does it have to say about anti-Semitism? How would you answer the charge that Shakespeare himself must have been anti-Semitic to present such a villainous Jew? (Look back at the activities on pages 32, 118, 125, 130.)

(f) How many different kinds of love relationship does the play present? Would you include Shylock and Jessica, for example? Or Antonio and Bassanio? How many of these relationships are one-sided? What kind of marriage do Lorenzo and Jessica have? Think about the ways in which love is explored in the play and how its effects are contrasted with the effects of hatred. (Look back at the activities on pages 81, 160.)

15 Ⓐ *A theme collage*

Draw a spider diagram which includes all the references you can find to one of the themes in the play. Then create a collage which illustrates how the theme is developed and explored.

Ⓑ *Discussing a theme*

Look back at the activities on one of the themes and write about:
• how the theme is developed and explored in the play
• what it adds to your overall interpretation of the play's meanings.

Ⓒ *Analysing the themes*

Write an account of the themes in *The Merchant of Venice*, showing how the themes are developed and the key words recur, to contribute to the overall meanings of the play.

Plot review

16 **Ⓐ** *Newspaper headlines*

Write a series of headlines that might have appeared in *The Rialto*, to accompany articles on the Antonio–Shylock story. Start with the day on which Jessica is reported to have eloped with Lorenzo and finish after the trial.

Ⓑ *Radio reports*

Write a series of brief radio reports which might have been broadcast over Radio Venice, covering all the main events portrayed in the play. Each one should be no more than two or three sentences long, but should summarise the most important news of the day. (You should include Jessica's elopement with a Christian, for example, the reported loss of Antonio's ships and Bassanio's successful visit to Belmont.) If possible, record one or two of your reports and include brief interviews where appropriate.

Ⓒ *A television programme*

How might a serious television current affairs programme in Venice have handled the events leading up to and during the trial? Draft the script for a programme which includes a feature on the background to the trial, factual reports from a courtroom correspondent and interviews with appropriate people (such as the Duke or Tubal). Finally, perform the script.

17 Re-tell either Portia's or Shylock's story as:

Ⓐ *Acrostic*

a 'MERCHANT OF VENICE' acrostic (in this case, a 16-line poem, the first line beginning with M, then E, then R... and so on)

Ⓑ *Mini-saga*

a prose story of exactly fifty words, no more, no less

Ⓒ *Sonnet*

similar to the one spoken by the Chorus in *Romeo and Juliet* or at the end of *Henry V.*

Acting

- There was very little rehearsal time, with several plays 'in repertory' (being performed) in any given period.
- We don't actually know about the style of acting, but modern, naturalistic, low-key acting was probably not possible on the Globe stage. At the same time, Shakespeare appears to be mocking over-the-top delivery in at least two of his plays.

Read *Hamlet* 3.2 (Hamlet's first three speeches to the First Player) and *A Midsummer Night's Dream* (especially Act 5).

- Actors certainly needed to be aware of their relationship with the audience: there must have been plenty of direct contact. In a daylight theatre there can be no pretence that the audience is not there.

Publishing

- Plays were not really regarded as 'literature' in Shakespeare's lifetime, and so the playwright would not have been interested in publishing his plays in book form.
- Some of Shakespeare's plays were, however, originally printed in cheap 'quarto' (pocket-size) editions. Some were sold officially (under an agreement made between the theatre company and the author), and some pirated (frequently by the actors themselves who had learned most of the script by heart).
- In 1623, seven years after Shakespeare's death, two of his close friends, John Heminge (or Heminges) and Henry Condell, collected together the most reliable versions of the plays and published them in a larger size volume known as the **First Folio**. This included eighteen plays which had never before appeared in print, and eighteen more which had appeared in quarto editions. Only *Pericles* was omitted from the plays which make up what we nowadays call Shakespeare's 'Complete Works' (unless we count plays such as *Two Noble Kinsmen*, which Shakespeare is known to have written with another writer, and *Edward III*, which some people claim to be by Shakespeare).

Much of the information in these sections comes from Michael Mangan, *A Preface to Shakespeare's Comedies: 1594–1603*, Longman, 1996.

The Globe Theatre

No one knows precisely what Shakespeare's Globe theatre looked like, but we do have a number of clues:

- a section of the foundations has been unearthed and provides a good idea of the size and shape of the outside walls
- the foundations of **the Rose**, a theatre near Shakespeare's, have been completely excavated
- a Dutch visitor to Shakespeare's London called Johannes de Witt saw a play in the Swan theatre and made a sketch of the interior (see below).

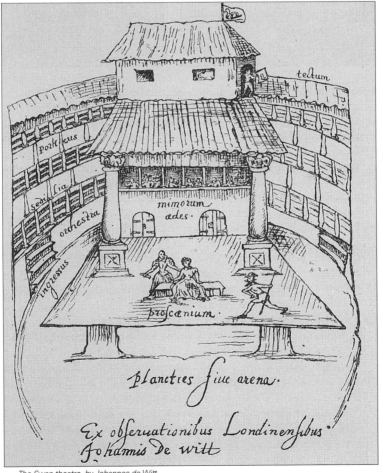

The Swan theatre, by Johannes de Witt

Background to Shakespeare and *The Merchant of Venice*

Using all the evidence available, a reconstruction of Shakespeare's Globe theatre has been built in London, not far from the site of the original building.

Ⓐ *The facts*

From what you can learn from these photographs:

1. Roughly what shape is the theatre, looked at from above?
2. How many storeys does it have?
3. In which areas can the audience (a) stand and (b) sit?
4. What is behind the stage?
5. How much scenery and lighting are used?
6. What other details can you pick out which seem to make the Globe different from an indoor theatre (which has a stage at one end, similar to many school assembly halls)?

Ⓑ *Using the stage*

Copy the plan on page 199. Then, using the staging guidelines provided, sketch or mark characters as they might appear at crucial moments in *The Merchant of Venice* (such as the moment when Shylock is about to cut Antonio's flesh in 5.1.).

Ⓒ *The actor–audience relationship*

- In what ways is the design of Shakespeare's Globe ideally suited to the performance of his plays?
- How might the open stage and the balcony be useful? (Refer to moments in *The Merchant of Venice* or other Shakespeare plays that you know.)
- What do you think would be the most interesting features of the way in which Shakespeare's actors – and those on the reconstructed Globe today – might relate to and interact with the audience? (Which moments in *The Merchant of Venice* seem to require a performance in which the audience are very close to the actors, for example?)

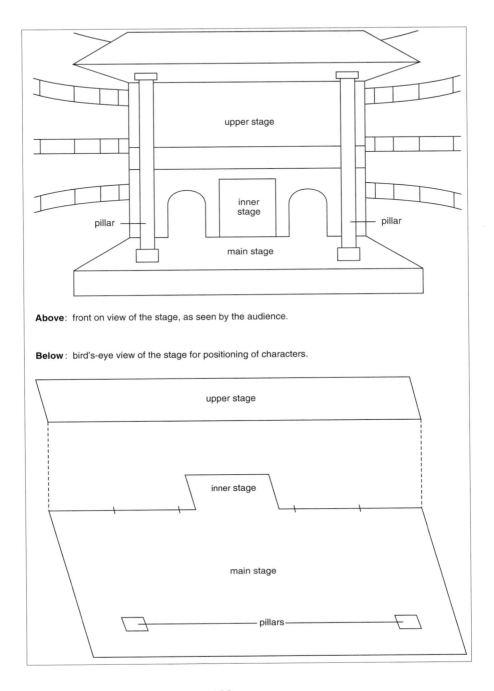

Above: front on view of the stage, as seen by the audience.

Below: bird's-eye view of the stage for positioning of characters.

of the ghetto. Each Jew was also required to wear a yellow spot on his back, or, if that was covered up, a yellow hat or turban (later changed to red). Many of these restrictions, however, were lifted during Shakespeare's lifetime and there is no doubt that Venice benefited greatly from its Jewish population, not only in helping to build the city's reputation for learning, but as money-lenders to the poor, and as successful merchants who brought a great deal of trade to the city.

In the twentieth century, however, the Venetian name for its Jewish quarter, *ghetto*, has come to be used for any over-populated district to which its residents are restricted, and is understood as a symbol of persecution and segregation.

Usury

During Shakespeare's lifetime there was much fierce debate about the acceptability of lending money for interest (usury). It was condemned by the Christian church and many people considered that, whereas making money through trade was virtuous, usury was immoral because it allowed someone to make money without working for it. The arguments for and against are set out in a famous essay by Shakespeare's contemporary, Sir Francis Bacon, titled 'On Usury'. Among other things, Bacon points out that, whatever people say publicly, usury is extremely common and no European government could exist without recourse to money-lenders. Shakespeare himself would have had views on the subject: his company built the Globe with borrowed money and found the repayment with interest extremely difficult.

The literary background

The Book of Genesis

Genesis is the first book in the Old Testament of the Bible and gives a version of the creation of the universe and the early history of humankind. It includes the story of Jacob, the great ancestor of the Jewish people, a figure referred to more than once in *The Merchant of Venice*.

Chapter 32 of Genesis (verse 10) tells how Jacob began as a poor man, his only possession a staff (see 2.5.36). Chapters 27 and 30 relate the story of Jacob and his brother Esau. Esau should have inherited the land from his father, Isaac, and would thereby have become the 'third possessor' (1.3.70) after his grandfather Abraham; but Rebecca, Jacob's 'wise mother' (1.3.69) helped Jacob to cheat his brother out of the inheritance by deceiving his father Isaac, who was blind. Later, when he was working for his father-in-law Laban, Jacob cunningly persuaded the old man to let him take all the lambs which are born 'streaked and pied' (1.3.75). Shakespeare's audience would have been extremely familiar with these stories and it was the general belief at that time that Jacob was guilty of dishonest practices.

The Jew of Malta

Christopher Marlowe's play *The Jew of Malta* was written around 1590 and Shakespeare must have known it very well. Its central character is a Jew called Barabas, who tells us openly about his wicked deeds:

> I walk abroad o' nights
> And kill sick people groaning under the walls;
> Sometimes I go about and poison wells...

Like Shylock, Barabas is a money-lender, obtaining money by threats, cheating and heavy penalty payments:

> Then after that I was an usurer,
> And with extorting, cozening, forfeiting,
> And tricks belonging unto brokery,
> I fill'd the jails with bankrupts in a year,
> And with young orphans planted hospitals,
> And every moon made some or other mad,
> And now and then one hang himself for grief,
> Pinning upon his breast a long great scroll
> How I with interest tormented him.

It is difficult to say how far Shakespeare was influenced by Marlowe, or in what ways; but you only have to look at Shylock and Barabas together to see how very different the two characters – and the two plays – are.

Iambic pentameter

A foot which contains an unstressed syllable followed by a stressed one (the standard 'beat': dee-**dum**) is called an 'iamb'. Verse which has five iambs per line as its standard rhythm is called 'iambic pentameter'.

Iambic pentameter which does not rhyme is also sometimes known as 'blank verse'.

1. Bearing in mind that the iambic pentameter line goes: dee-**dum**, dee-**dum**, dee-**dum**, dee-**dum**, dee-**dum**, make up some of your own 'Shakespearean' verse (perhaps based on one of the themes of the play, such as love).
2. Copy out the following lines from 4.1 and divide them into five feet; then mark the heavy stresses:
   16, 36, 70, 84 and (more difficult) 85.
3. Do the same with these key lines: 1.3.42, 1.3.177, 3.2.74, 4.1.180, 4.1.302. Pick one and show how the rhythm helps the meaning.

Rhyme

Shakespeare sometimes uses rhyme for the ends of scenes, where a 'rhyming couplet' can have the effect of rounding things off, as it does in 1.1.

Find other scenes which end with a rhyming couplet and discuss what the effect might be in each case.

Verse and prose

It is never totally clear why Shakespeare chooses to write some scenes, or passages, in verse, and others in prose.

Although there are many examples where the more serious scenes, involving great passions, are in verse while those about ordinary people and comedy are in prose, there are also significant examples throughout Shakespeare's plays where this is not the case. Shylock's famous 'Hath not a Jew...' speech (in 3.1) is a good example of an impassioned character speaking in prose.

Look back through *The Merchant of Venice* and try to work out why certain scenes are in verse and others in prose.

The plot of *The Merchant of Venice*

Act 1

1.1: When the play opens, Salerio and Solanio are asking their friend Antonio why he is sad; he claims not to be worried about the safety of his ships and the rich cargoes they carry, and also denies that he is sad because he is in love. Salerio and Solanio leave when other friends arrive – Bassanio, Lorenzo and Gratiano. Gratiano attempts to cheer Antonio up and advises him not to be one of those people who put on a serious expression and remain silent, merely to look clever and wise.

When he is left alone with Bassanio, Antonio asks his friend about the woman he had promised to tell him about. Opening his story with a reminder of all the money he owes, Bassanio says that he has a plan which will enable him to pay off his debts; and he begins to tell Antonio about the rich, beautiful and virtuous Portia, who lives in Belmont.

Antonio explains that, although all his own money is tied up in trading investments, he is willing to borrow the amount that Bassanio needs to finance his trip to Belmont.

1.2: In Belmont we meet Portia. She is depressed because her dead father's will prevents her from choosing a husband; instead, any man who wants to marry her has to pick one of three caskets – gold, silver or lead: whoever chooses the right one can claim her hand. Her lady-in-waiting Nerissa goes through the list of the current suitors and Portia mocks each one, before Nerissa reveals – much to Portia's relief – that they have all decided to pull out of the contest and return home. Portia has fond memories of a young Venetian who once visited the house, called Bassanio, but is not pleased to hear that a new suitor is on his way: the Prince of Morocco.

1.3: Back in Venice, Bassanio approaches the money-lender Shylock for a loan of three thousand ducats. Shylock expresses some concerns about the safety of Antonio's investments, but agrees to think seriously about entering into a contract to lend him the money. When Antonio arrives, Shylock tells the audience how much he hates him and why. Antonio has often insulted Shylock in public because he is a Jew and a money-lender, and Shylock vows to get his revenge if he can.

3.2: Bassanio has arrived in Belmont. Portia is anxious for him to take time before making his choice, but he is in torment and wants to get it over with. Comparing Bassanio with the hero Hercules on one of his great exploits, Portia orders a song to be sung while he makes his choice and anxiously stands aside as he approaches the caskets. After thinking seriously about the inscriptions, Bassanio realises that appearances can often be deceptive and chooses the lead casket, rejecting the superficial attractiveness of gold and silver. Portia is ecstatic as Bassanio finds her portrait inside with a scroll telling him that he can claim her as his wife. Telling Bassanio that she and all her wealth and possessions are now his, Portia gives him a ring, saying that, if he ever loses it or gives it away, it will mean that he has stopped loving her.

Gratiano and Nerissa offer their delighted congratulations and then reveal that they themselves have fallen in love and want to get married, but, as the two couples are sharing a joke, Lorenzo, Jessica and Salerio arrive from Venice.

Bassanio is shocked when he reads a letter from Antonio, and he tells Portia about his debts to Antonio, the bond with Shylock and the loss of Antonio's ships. Salerio confirms the account of Antonio's losses and reports that Shylock is demanding justice, determined to wreak his revenge. Portia offers to pay Shylock much more than he is owed and tells Bassanio to set off for Venice in order to settle the debt; but, before he leaves, he reads her Antonio's letter.

3.3: In Venice, Antonio has persuaded the gaoler to let him come out of prison to approach Shylock; but Shylock will not listen to pleas for mercy and storms off, determined to exact the penalty of a pound of Antonio's flesh. Antonio faces defeat, knowing that the Duke will not be able to bend the law just to let him off the hook.

3.4: In Belmont, Lorenzo praises Portia for encouraging Bassanio to go to Antonio's aid, and she temporarily hands over control of her house to Lorenzo and Jessica, explaining that she and Nerissa are planning to stay in a nearby monastery until their husbands return. Portia then sends her servant Balthazar to Padua with a letter for her lawyer cousin, Doctor Bellario, asking for some law books and courtroom dress. She plans to disguise herself and Nerissa as young male lawyers and journey to Venice in an attempt to help Antonio.

3.5: Launcelot warns Jessica that she might be damned for being a Jew's daughter. She reminds him that, in marrying Lorenzo, she has become a Christian, and her husband enters just as Launcelot is complaining that all these Jews converting to Christianity are putting up the price of pork and bacon! Lorenzo accuses Launcelot of having got one of the servants pregnant; and, after repeatedly (and deliberately) misunderstanding Lorenzo's instructions, Launcelot goes in to arrange the serving of dinner. Jessica tells Lorenzo how much she admires Portia and the couple go in to dinner, joking with each other.

Act 4

4.1: In the Duke's palace, Antonio presents himself before the court and the Duke expresses his sympathy. When Shylock enters, the Duke tries to persuade him to show mercy and drop the case against Antonio, but he rejects the Duke's pleas and explains why he is pursuing the case: he has sworn an oath to exact the penalty, he says, and he refuses to give any reason for his actions, other than his hatred for Antonio. Shylock rejects Bassanio's offer of twice the sum owed and argues that his demand for a pound of Antonio's flesh is a fair one, in line with the laws of Venice.

As Antonio is claiming to be resigned to his death, Nerissa arrives, disguised as a lawyer's clerk, with a letter from Doctor Bellario. Meanwhile Gratiano expresses his disgust at Shylock, who is sharpening his knife in preparation for cutting off the flesh, but Shylock remains unmoved by Gratiano's insults. The Duke reads out Bellario's letter: he is ill, but in his place he has sent a young lawyer called Balthazar, who understands all about the case. Portia enters, disguised as the lawyer, and opens the case by asking Shylock to be merciful. She explains the true nature of mercy and its power to soften the harshness of stark justice; mercy is the only thing that can save people from damnation, she argues. But Shylock refuses to budge.

When Bassanio asks the Duke to bend the law to save Antonio, and Portia objects, saying that it would have a bad effect on future cases, Shylock praises her wisdom and skill as a lawyer.

In response to Portia's final questions, Shylock presents the set of balances he has ready to weigh out the flesh, but declares that he has not arranged for a surgeon to stand by, as there is no provision for it in the bond. Antonio takes a loving farewell of Bassanio, claiming to be glad that he will not have to live on in poverty and asking that Portia should be told about his love for his young friend.

Just as Shylock is about to use his knife on Antonio, Portia stops him: he can take the flesh, she warns, but the bond says nothing about blood: if he sheds one drop of blood, all his lands and goods will be confiscated. Shylock is stunned; and instantly accepts the offer of three times the sum owed; but Portia stands firm – he must take the flesh and accept the consequences. But now she adds a further condition: on penalty of losing his own life, Shylock must take exactly a pound – no more, no less.

Shylock realises that he is defeated and tries to leave, but Portia stops him with another law. As a Jew, Shylock is considered an 'alien'; and if an alien plots to kill a Venetian, half his wealth can be confiscated by the state and the other half given to the victim. He also stands to be executed. The Duke shows mercy: the state will not take half Shylock's money, but merely fine him; and Antonio is willing to forget the fine, so long as he can have the other half of Shylock's wealth, to give to Lorenzo when Shylock dies. But there are two conditions: first, that Shylock must become a Christian; second that Shylock must agree to leave the rest of his wealth and any future earnings to Lorenzo after his death. Shylock agrees and leaves the court.

The Duke thanks 'Balthazar' and Bassanio offers 'him' the three thousand ducats owed to Shylock. Portia refuses the money, but, when pressed to accept some gift, asks for Bassanio's ring – the one she had given him as a love-token. He refuses and she leaves, pretending to be offended. Concerned not to seem ungrateful, Antonio persuades Bassanio to give the ring to the young lawyer and Bassanio reluctantly sends Gratiano in pursuit.

4.2: Out in the street, Portia politely accepts the gift when Gratiano catches up with them, and Nerissa decides to test her husband, by seeing if she can persuade him to part with his ring too.

Act 5

5.1: In Belmont Lorenzo and Jessica are recalling lovers from classical mythology who met on moonlit nights such as this one, when Stephano, one of Portia's servants, arrives. He reports that Portia is expected home before dawn and Launcelot then enters to say that a messenger has brought news that Bassanio will be back at the same time. Lorenzo and Jessica sit down, watching the stars. Lorenzo asks the musicians to play and he talks about the power of music.

As Portia and Nerissa approach they see the light shining from the house and hear the music. Lorenzo recognises Portia's voice and welcomes her back with the news that Bassanio and Gratiano are expected any minute. Portia orders that no one is to reveal that she has been away.

Portia greets Bassanio when he arrives and then welcomes Antonio, but a quarrel breaks out between Nerissa and Gratiano: she accuses him of having given his ring away to a woman and refuses to believe his story that he gave it to the judge's clerk. Portia takes Nerissa's side, saying that Bassanio would never give her ring away! But when Gratiano spills the beans, Portia reproaches her husband, pointing out how important the ring was as a symbol of their love and claiming that Nerissa is right: the rings were given away to women! Bassanio tries in vain to explain why he felt obliged to give the ring to the young lawyer, but Portia and Nerissa threaten to take their revenge: they will have sex with the lawyer and his clerk if ever they visit Belmont.

When Antonio speaks up in support of his friend, Portia relents and hands him another ring to give to Bassanio. When he looks at the ring, Bassanio is amazed to find that it is the same one and, after the women have teased their husbands by pretending that were given the rings by the lawyer and his clerk as a reward for their sexual favours, Portia reveals the truth. She also tells Antonio that three of his ships have returned safely, and in the general amazement, hands Lorenzo the document which ensures him of all Shylock's wealth on his death. They go indoors to hear the full story from Portia.

Study skills: titles and quotations

Referring to titles

When you are writing an essay, you will often need to refer to the title of the play. There are two main ways of doing this:

- If you are hand-writing your essay, the title of the play should be underlined: <u>The Merchant of Venice</u>
- If you are word-processing your essay, the play title should be in italics: *The Merchant of Venice*.

The same rules apply to titles of all plays and other long works including novels and non-fiction, such as: *Animal Farm* and *The Diary of Anne Frank*. The titles of poems or short stories are placed inside single inverted commas; for example: 'Timothy Winters' and 'A Sound of Thunder'.

Note that the first word in a title and all the main words will have capital (or 'upper case') letters, while the less important words (such as conjunctions, prepositions and articles) will usually begin with lower case letters; for example: *The Taming of the Shrew* or *Antony and Cleopatra*.

Using quotations

Quotations show that you know the play in detail and are able to produce evidence from the script to back up your ideas and opinions. It is usually a good idea to keep quotations as short as you can (and this especially applies to exams, where it is a waste of time copying chunks out of the script).

Using longer quotations

There are a number of things you should do if you want to use a quotation of more than a few words:

1. Make your point. ——— *We cannot ignore Shylock's threat:* ——— 2. A colon introduces the quotation.

3. Leave a line. ———

4. Indent the quotation. ——— *If I can catch him once upon the hip,* ——— 5. No quotation marks.
  I will feed the ancient grudge I bear him.

6. Keep the same line divisions as the script.

7. Continue with a ——— *Here he seems to be...*
follow-up point, perhaps commenting on the quotation itself.

Using brief quotations

Brief quotations are usually easier to use, take less time to write out and are much more effective in showing how familiar you are with the play. Weave them into the sentence like this:

- Describing himself as 'a tainted wether of the flock', Antonio seems to be...

If you are asked to state where the quotation comes from, use this simple form of reference to indicate the Act, scene and line:

- Recognising that 'The world is still deceived with ornament' (3.2.74), Bassanio...

In some editions this is written partly in Roman numerals – upper case for the Act and lower case for the scene; for example: (II.i.81), or (II.1.81).

William Shakespeare and *The Merchant of Venice*

We do not know exactly when Shakespeare wrote *The Merchant of Venice*, but it must have been before 1598, when a man called Francis Meres listed it among the plays that Shakespeare was known to have written.

Shakespeare's life and career

No one is absolutely sure when Shakespeare wrote each play.

1564 Born in Stratford-upon-Avon, first son of John and Mary Shakespeare.

1582 Marries Anne Hathaway from the nearby village of Shottery. She is 8 years older and expecting their first child.

1583 Daughter Susannah born.

1585 Twin son and daughter, Hamnet and Judith, born.

Some time before **1592** Shakespeare arrives in London, becomes an actor and writes poems and plays. Several plays are performed, probably including the three parts of *Henry VI*. Another writer, Robert Greene, writes about 'Shake-scene', the 'upstart crow' who has clearly become a popular playwright.

By **1595** he is a shareholder with the Lord Chamberlain's Men (see page 195) and has probably written *Richard III*, *Comedy of Errors*, *Titus Andronicus*, *The Taming of the Shrew*, *The Two Gentlemen of Verona*, *Love's Labours Lost*, *Romeo and Juliet*, *Richard II* and *A Midsummer Night's Dream* (as well as contributing to plays by other writers and writing the poems 'Venus and Adonis' and 'The Rape of Lucrece').

1596 Hamnet dies, age 11.

1597 Buys New Place, one of the finest houses in Stratford.

1599 Globe Theatre opens on Bankside.

By **1599**: *King John*, *The Merchant of Venice*, the two parts of *Henry IV*, *The Merry Wives of Windsor*, *Much Ado About Nothing*, *Julius Caesar* and *Henry V* (as well as the Sonnets).

1603 King James I grants the Lord Chamberlain's Men a Royal Patent and they become The King's Men (page 195).

By **1608**: *As You Like It*, *Hamlet*, *Twelfth Night*, *Troilus and Cressida*, *All's Well That Ends Well*, *Measure For Measure*, *Othello*, *Macbeth*, *King Lear*, *Antony and Cleopatra*, *Pericles*, *Coriolanus* and *Timon of Athens*.

1608 The King's Men begin performing plays in the indoor Blackfriars Theatre (page 195).

By **1613**: *Cymbeline*, *The Winter's Tale*, *The Tempest*, *Henry VIII*, *Two Noble Kinsmen* (the last two probably with John Fletcher).

1616 Dies, April 23, and is buried in Holy Trinity Church, Stratford.

1623 Publication of the First Folio (page 196).

Shakespeare's times

1558 Elizabeth I becomes queen.

1565 The explorer John Hawkins introduces sweet potatoes and tobacco into England.

1567 Mary Queen of Scots abdicates in favour of her year-old son, James VI.

1568 Mary escapes to England and is imprisoned by Elizabeth.

1572 Francis Drake attacks Spanish ports in the Americas.

1576 James Burbage opens the first theatre (The Theatre) in London.

1580 Francis Drake returns from a circumnavigation of the world.

1582 Pope Gregory reforms the Christian calendar.

1587 Mary Queen of Scots executed for a treasonous plot against Elizabeth; Drake partly destroys the Spanish fleet at Cádiz and war breaks out with Spain.

1588 Philip II of Spain's Armada is destroyed by the English fleet.

1592 Plague kills 20,000 Londoners.

1593 Playwright Christopher Marlowe killed in a pub brawl.

1596 Tomatoes introduced into England; John Harington invents the water-closet (the ancestor of the modern lavatory).

1597 Earl of Tyrone leads a new rebellion in Ireland.

1599 Earl of Essex concludes a truce with Tyrone, returns home and is arrested.

1601 Essex is tried and executed for treasonous plots against Elizabeth.

1603 Elizabeth I dies and is succeeded by James VI of Scotland as James I of England.
Sir Walter Raleigh is jailed for plotting against James.

1604 James is proclaimed 'King of Great Britain, France and Ireland'; new church rules cause 300 Puritan clergy to resign.

1605 Gunpowder Plot uncovered.

1607 First permanent European settlement in America at Jamestown, Virginia.

1610 Galileo looks at the stars through a telescope; tea is introduced into Europe.

1611 Authorised Version of the Bible.

1618 Raleigh executed for treason.
Physician William Harvey announces discovery of blood circulation.

1620 Pilgrim Fathers sail from Plymouth to colonise America.

1625 James I dies and is succeeded by Charles I.

Index to activities

Index to activities